T4-ALH-094

Common WordPerfect 6 for Windows Features

Feature	How to Get There	Feature	How to Get There
Figure (retrieve)	Alt+G F	Graphics Box (edit)	Double-click graphics box
File (insert)	Alt+I I	Graphics Line	Alt+G L
File Management	Ctrl+O, F3 or F4	Graphics Line (edit)	Double-click line
File Name (insert in text)	Alt+I OF	Hanging Indent	Ctrl+F7
Files (default location)	Alt+F E Alt+F ↵	Hard Page Break	Ctrl+↵
Find, Find Next, Find Previous	F2, Shift+F2, Alt+F2 respectively	Hard Space	Ctrl+space
		Header/Footer	Alt+L H
Floating cell	F12 F	Help	Alt+H or F1 or Shift+F1
Flush Right (all lines)	Ctrl+R	Hypertext	Alt+T H
Flush Right (line)	Alt+F7	Hyphenation	Alt+L LE
		Indent	F7
Fonts and Font Attributes	F9	Index	Alt+T X
Footnote	Alt+I F	Info (document)	Alt+F I
Full Justification (all lines)	Alt+L JA	Initial Codes Style	Alt+L DS
Full Justification (paragraph)	Ctrl+J	Insert/ Typeover	Ins
		Italics	Ctrl+I
Generate Auto-References	Ctrl+F9	Keep Text Together	Alt+L PK
Go To	Ctrl+G	Labels	Alt+L B
Grammar	Alt+Shift+F1	Left Justification (all lines)	Ctrl+L
Graphics Box	Alt+G then F, T,Q, or C		

The SYBEX Instant Reference Series

Instant References are available on these topics:

AutoCAD Release 12 for DOS

AutoCAD Release 12 for Windows

CorelDRAW 3

CorelDRAW 4

dBASE

dBASE IV 2.0 Programmer's

DOS 5

DOS 6

DR DOS 6

Excel 4 for Windows

Harvard Graphics 3

Harvard Graphics for Windows

Lotus 1-2-3 Release 2.3 & 2.4 for DOS

Lotus 1-2-3 Release 4 for Windows

Lotus 1-2-3 for Windows

Microsoft Access

Norton Desktop for DOS

Norton Desktop for Windows 2.0

Norton Utilities 7

OS/2 2.1

PageMaker 4.0 for the Macintosh

Paradox 4 Programmer's

Paradox 4 User's

Paradox for Windows User's

PC Tools 8

Quattro Pro for Windows

SQL

Windows 3.1

Windows NT

Word for Windows, Version 2.0

WordPerfect 5.1 for DOS

WordPerfect 5.1 for Windows

WordPerfect 6 for DOS

Computer users are not all alike.
Neither are SYBEX books.

We know our customers have a variety of needs. They've told us so. And because we've listened, we've developed several distinct types of books to meet the needs of each of our customers. What are you looking for in computer help?

If you're looking **for the basics, try the ABC's series. For a more visual approa**ch, select full-color **Quick & Easy** books.

Running Start books are two books in one: a fast-paced tutorial, followed by a command reference.

Mastering and **Understanding** titles offer you a step-by-step introduction, plus an in-depth examination of intermediate-level features, to use as you progress.

Our **Up & Running** series is designed for computer-literate consumers who want a no-nonsense overview of new programs. Just 20 basic lessons, and you're on your way.

SYBEX **Encyclopedias, Desktop References**, and **A to Z** books provide a comprehensive reference and explanation of all of the commands, features, and functions of the subject software.

Sometimes a subject requires a special treatment that our standard series don't provide. So you'll find we have titles like **Advanced Techniques, Handbooks, Tips & Tricks,** and others that are specifically tailored to satisfy a unique need.

You'll find SYBEX publishes a variety of books on every popular software package. Looking for computer help? Help Yourself to SYBEX.

For a complete catalog of our publications:

SYBEX SYBEX Inc.
2021 Challenger Drive, Alameda, CA 94501
Tel: (510) 523-8233/(800) 227-2346 Telex: 336311
Fax: (510) 523-2373

SYBEX is committed to using natural resources wisely to preserve and improve our environment. This is why we have been printing the text of books like this one on recycled paper since 1982.

This year our use of recycled paper will result in the saving of more than 15,300 trees. We will lower air pollution effluents by 54,000 pounds, save 6,300,000 gallons of water, and reduce landfill by 2,700 cubic yards.

In choosing a SYBEX book you are not only making a choice for the best in skills and information, you are also choosing to enhance the quality of life for all of us.

WordPerfect® 6 for Windows™ Instant Reference

Alan Simpson

San Francisco • Paris • Düsseldorf • Soest

Developmental Editors: Steve Lipson, Sarah Wadsworth
Editor: Michelle Nance
Technical Editors: Sheila Dienes, Erik Ingenito
Assistant Editors: Kris Vanberg-Wolff, Valerie Potter
Production Editor: Carolina Montilla
Book Designer: Ingrid Owen
Production Artist: Lisa Jaffe
Screen Graphics: Cuong Le
Desktop Publishing Specialist: Stephanie Hollier
Indexer: Nancy Guenther
Cover Designer: Archer Design
Cover Photographer: Mark Johann
Cover Photograph Art Direction: Ingalls + Associates
Screen reproductions produced with Collage Plus
Collage Plus is a trademark of Inner Media Inc.

SYBEX is a registered trademark of SYBEX Inc.

TRADEMARKS: SYBEX has attempted throughout this book to
distinguish proprietary trademarks from descriptive terms by following the capitalization style used by the manufacturer.

SYBEX is not affiliated with any manufacturer.

Every effort has been made to supply complete and accurate information. However, SYBEX assumes no responsibility for its use,
nor for any infringement of the intellectual property rights of
third parties which would result from such use.

Copyright ©1994 SYBEX Inc., 2021 Challenger Drive, Alameda,
CA 94501. World rights reserved. No part of this publication may
be stored in a retrieval system, transmitted, or reproduced in any
way, including but not limited to photocopy, photograph, mag-
netic or other record, without the prior agreement and written
permission of the publisher.

Library of Congress Card Number: 93-86068

ISBN: 0-7821-1383-4

Manufactured in the United States of America

10 9 8 7 6 5 4 3 2

To Susan, Ashley, and Alec

Acknowledgments

Every book is a team effort, and this one is certainly no exception. The skills, talents, and hard work of many people brought this book from the idea stage into your hands.

On the publishing side the following people were instrumental in creating this book: Sarah Wadsworth, developmental editor; Michelle Nance, editor; Sheila Dienes and Erik Ingenito, technical editors; Kris Vanberg-Wolff and Valerie Potter, assistant editors; Carolina Montilla, Production Editor; Lisa Jaffe, artist; Cuong Le, screen graphics; and Stephanie Hollier, typesetter.

On the authorial side, the talented writers Elizabeth Olson and Martha Mellor provided most of the material in this book; Martha Mellor miraculously managed to put it all together.

Thanks to Bill Gladstone and Matt Wagner of Waterside Production for handling business matters.

Susan, Ashley, and Alec provided love, support, sustenance, comfort, and lots of patience.

Table of Contents

Introduction

xiii

FEATURES
(LISTED ALPHABETICALLY)

Index

Introduction

WordPerfect Corporation has taken all the best features of the graphical user interface and incorporated them beautifully into their version 6.0 of the now-legendary WordPerfect word processing program. Both beginners and old hands alike will appreciate the intuitive, interactive means of creating and editing documents that WordPerfect 6.0 for Windows brings to the personal computer.

WHO SHOULD READ THIS BOOK

This book is designed for WordPerfect users who are on the go. Its portable yet comprehensive format provides ready access to all those big features and little details that are so easily forgotten. Of course, the compact size does not allow for lengthy tutorials about every feature, so if you're new to WordPerfect for Windows, you may want to back this book up with a more comprehensive tutorial, such as *Mastering WordPerfect 6 for Windows*, also published by SYBEX.

HOW TO USE THIS BOOK

This book is organized as an encyclopedic reference, with topics arranged alphabetically. Each reference section includes (as appropriate):

- A general description of the feature
- Step-by-step instructions for the use of the feature
- Notes providing additional usage tips and suggestions
- Cross-references to related topics and features

To speed things along, we often present a series of menu selections with an arrow (➤) separating each option and the optional letter choice for each option underlined. If the command has a shortcut key sequence, we'll present it in parentheses, like this:

Choose Layout ➤ Margins (Ctrl+F8).

You can use any of the usual Windows techniques—the mouse, the arrow keys, or the keyboard—for choosing menu options. If you are not already familiar with these techniques, perhaps your best starting point would be to refer to the "Mouse" and "Menus" sections in this book.

SYSTEM REQUIREMENTS

To use WordPerfect for Windows, your computer must have the following hardware and software configuration:

- An 80386SX or higher processor
- At *least* 8MB Random Access Memory (WordPerfect can run on 4MB, but it will be very slow)
- A graphics adapter supporting standard VGA, Super VGA, or Hercules graphics
- A hard disk with at least 33MB available storage for a standard (full) installation, or about 11MB for a minimum installation
- Either a 3.5" (1.44MB) or a 5.25" (1.2MB) floppy disk drive
- Windows version 3.1 configured to run in 386 Enhanced mode.
- DOS version 3.0 or higher

Though not essential, a mouse is highly recommended, since some features are not accessible without one.

INSTALLING WORDPERFECT FOR WINDOWS

Like any software product, WordPerfect for Windows needs to be installed on your computer before you can use it (you need only install the program once). To install WordPerfect for Windows:

1. Start your computer normally, and then start Windows.
2. Insert the WordPerfect 6.0 for Windows Install 1 disk into drive A or B.
3. From the Windows Program Manager, choose File ➤ Run.

4. Type **A:INSTALL** (or **B:INSTALL**, if the disk is in drive B) and press ↵.

5. You'll be prompted for your name and license number, which is printed on the Certificate of License registration card that came with your WordPerfect for Windows package. Choose <u>C</u>ontinue.

6. Follow the instructions that appear on your screen. (You can choose <u>S</u>tandard when given the option to install the entire program on drive C.)

STARTING WORDPERFECT FOR WINDOWS

To start WordPerfect for Windows, you can either type **WIN WPWIN** and press ↵ at the DOS command prompt, or

1. Start Windows in the usual manner (by typing **win**).

2. Double-click the WPWIN 6.0 group icon in the Program Manager window.

3. Double-click the WPWIN 6.0 program item icon in the group window.

WORDPERFECT KEYBOARDS

In this book, we assume that you will be using the default WPWIN 6.0 Keyboard. *If you have any problems duplicating the instructions presented in this book, it may be that a keyboard other than the WordPerfect for Windows 6.0 keyboard is in use.* To switch back to the default keyboard:

1. Choose <u>F</u>ile ➤ Pr<u>e</u>ferences and double-click <u>K</u>eyboard.

2. Highlight <WPWIN 6.0 Keyboard> and choose <u>S</u>elect.

3. Choose <u>C</u>lose.

The WPWIN 6.0 keystrokes will then work properly, and the pull-down menus will show the appropriate shortcut keys.

WordPerfect 6.0's Hottest New Features

The section below summarizes some of the new and modified features in WordPerfect for Windows version 6.0. You can find additional information about each topic under the appropriate heading in the book.

Documents and Files

Improved File Manager, QuickList, and QuickFinder Streamlined file management tools make quick work of storing and finding files. You may never need the Windows File Manager again.

FAX and Mail

Fax If you have a compatible fax board, you can send a fax right from WordPerfect—there's no need to print the document first (see Print).

Send Mail from WordPerfect If you have network e-mail that's compatible with the Lotus VMI or Microsoft MAPI standard, you can send a document to somebody else without printing and without exiting WordPerfect.

Formatting/General

Abbreviations Type a shortcut word, symbol, or phrase into your document, then expand it automatically with the Abbreviations feature.

Bookmarks Find your place in a jiffy with QuickMark or create multiple BookMarks for your large documents.

Columns Working with columns is easier than ever, especially with the addition of optional built-in separator lines, borders, and Balanced Newspaper columns.

Counters WordPerfect has always incremented counters for graphics boxes automatically. Now you can also create your own counters to count anything you want, then increment and decrement them manually.

File and Path Names Insert the current file or path and file name anywhere in your document. This is especially handy in headers and footers.

Delay Codes Define headers, footers, and other repetitive elements at the top of the document and then delay the codes so they don't print until you get to a specific page.

Hidden Text Make selected portions of your document invisible and view or display the hidden text at will.

Initial Caps Quickly convert selected text to *UPPERCASE*, *lowercase*, or *Initial Caps* with Edit ➤ Convert Case.

Labels, Envelopes, Pamphlets, and Booklets Create these using enhanced and new features.

Outlines A special Outline feature bar makes creating and editing outlines a snap, and the outlines are collapsible now. You can also set up bulleted and numbered lists quickly with the Bullets & Numbers feature.

Find and Replace Find (and optionally replace) *specific codes*, such as particular fonts, throughout your document.

Graphics

Borders and Shading Draw borders around pages and paragraphs, and shade them if you like.

Contoured Text Countour text around the image that's *inside* **a graphics box, not just around the square box itself.**

Drop Shadows, Rounded Corners, Custom Lines Use predefined borders and lines to jazz up your documents. You can also customize borders and lines, set up rounded corners, and take complete control over the size, location, and color of drop shadows.

Drawing, Charting, and TextArt Full-featured drawing, charting, and text shaping packages are built right in.

Watermarks Print a light watermark on every page of your text.

Help

Coaches These aids let you learn a new feature while you work.

Tutorial Run the WordPerfect 6.0 tutorial right from your Help menu.

Information Sharing

Import Databases and Spreadsheets Import data from databases, spreadsheets, and ASCII delimited files into WordPerfect documents. You can link or import the data as a WordPerfect table, text file, or merge data file. Linked data is updated automatically if you change the underlying data file.

Launch Applications Automatically The Kickoff utility lets you launch applications anytime you want and repeat the launch at specified intervals.

Object Linking and Embedding WordPerfect supports Object Linking and Embedding (OLE) and Dynamic Data Exchange (DDE). These techniques let you put data created by other Windows applications into your WordPerfect documents. You can then view, play back, or edit the data without leaving WordPerfect. Changes to linked data are reflected in your WordPerfect document automatically.

Interactive Documents

Hypertext Use hypertext to build instant cross-referencing capability into a document, just like the jump words in a help screen. Jump to words, play sounds, roll a film clip—the capability is there!

Sound If you have a compatible sound card, you can make your on-screen documents talk, play music, or make any kind of sound.

Macros

Macro Command Language   The macro command language offers the capabilities of a real programming language and includes a command inserter to make programming jobs easier.

On-line Macro Reference   Choose Help ➤ Macros to access the extensive macro documentation available on disk.

Mass Mailings/Merges

Envelopes   Automatically create an envelope (with POSTNET bar codes) for every form letter you print.

POSTNET Bar Codes   Automatically print a POSTNET bar code on every mailing label or envelope to speed mail delivery.

Quick and Easy Merges   Use improved features to create a merge data file and fill it with data. When you reorganize or rename merge fields, WordPerfect adjusts the data automatically.

Store Merge Data in a Table   Say good-bye to those old "secondary merge files" with their weird coding. Now you can put merge data into a WordPerfect table.

Math

Built-in Spreadsheet   The Tables feature is now a complete spreadsheet. Use it to graph your data with the built-in Chart package; to do any kind of math, from financial calculations to trigonometry; and to enter formulas. You'll love the automatic Sum and Data Fill features.

Printing

Create a Booklet or Pamphlet   You can subdivide pages and then print them as a booklet. When printing is done, fold the pages in half and the booklet is ready for binding.

Print Preview is Gone   What you see is what you get! View and edit your document at any magnification, and display and edit facing pages (see Screen/Interface, below).

Screen/Interface

Power Bar and Feature Bars   A new *power bar* provides quick access to menu options. When you perform certain tasks, *feature bars* appear automatically. Click buttons in the feature bar to do any task quickly—no more scrounging around for the right menu options. The power bar, button bars, status bar, and menu bar are customizable.

Double-click Shortcuts   Double-click certain hot spots on the screen to go to relevant dialog boxes quickly.

QuickMenu Shortcuts   Right-clicking the mouse on a screen hot spot or object brings up a context-sensitive QuickMenu of options for the area you clicked. You no longer need to search through lengthy menus to find what you want.

Three View Modes   You can work and make changes in any of three different view modes: Draft, Page, or Two-Page. Page and Two-Page are WYSIWYG (what-you-see-is-what-you-get); Draft is an imitation. You can also display or hide bars, Reveal Codes, graphics boxes, hidden text, and white-space symbols.

What's It for?   Simply move your mouse pointer to a button, bar, menu option, or code. The WordPerfect title bar will tell you what that thing does.

Zoom   In Draft and Page view, you can zoom in for a close-up view or zoom out for an arm's-length view while editing your document.

Spelling and Document Information

Auto-Replace   Automatically replace common misspellings, such as replacing *hte* with *the*, without being prompted.

Dictionary Management   Design your own supplementary dictionaries and choose which dictionary will be updated with new words during a spell check. Supplementary dictionaries can include words to skip, replacement words, and alternative words.

Document Information   Get complete document statistics, not just a word count.

Styles and Templates

Put Anything in a Style   Styles can now include columns, graphics boxes, and even other styles.

Quick Format   Quickly copy formatting codes and Paragraph styles from one paragraph to others with the QuickFormat feature.

Style Libraries   Store styles in the current document, the current template, a supplemental template, or a separate style library file.

Templates   Templates define the initial appearance of new documents and the styles, macros, abbreviations, button bars, keyboards, and menus available when you edit them. Design your own templates or use one of the many supplied with WordPerfect.

Tables

Fancy Fills, Lines, and Drop Shadows   You no longer need to put a table in a graphics box to get these special effects.

Recalculate When You Want to   You can recalculate the current table or all tables in the document manually *or* automatically.

Spreadsheet   The built-in spreadsheet makes table math a breeze.

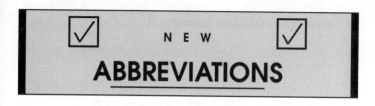

ABBREVIATIONS

It is sometimes easier to type an abbreviation or select it from a menu and have WordPerfect expand it for you than it is to type the whole word each time.

To Create an Abbreviation

1. Select the text you want to abbreviate.

2. Choose Insert ➤ Abbreviations, then choose Create from the Abbreviations dialog box.

3. Type an abbreviation for the selected text. The name is case-sensitive.

4. Choose OK, then choose Close to return to the document window.

Once you've set up an abbreviation, proceed as follows to insert the expanded form into your document:

1. Type the abbreviation (*exactly* as you typed it when creating the abbreviation) and place the cursor on the abbreviated text.

2. Press Ctrl+A.

If you prefer to expand an abbreviation without typing it first, follow these steps:

1. Position the cursor where you want the full text to appear.

2. Choose Insert ➤ Abbreviations to open the Abbreviations dialog box.

3. Double-click the abbreviation you want to expand, or highlight it and choose Expand.

To Delete an Abbreviation

1. Choose Insert ➤ Abbreviations and highlight the abbreviation you want to delete.

2. Choose Delete, answer Yes when asked for confirmation, and choose Close to return to your document.

To Copy an
Abbreviation to Another Template

1. Choose Insert ➤ Abbreviations.

2. Choose the Copy button. The Copy Abbreviation dialog box appears.

3. Select the template to copy from, the abbreviation you want to copy, and the template you want to copy to. Choose Copy.

NOTES You can also use the Find and Replace feature to expand abbreviated text.

SEE ALSO *Replace*

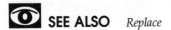

ADVANCE

Use Advance to move text to an exact horizontal and vertical position relative to the cursor or relative to the left and top edges of the page. Advance is often used to position the cursor in pre-printed forms.

To Position Text on the Page

1. Move the cursor to the page where you want to advance the text. If you want to advance text relative to the cursor position, place the cursor where you want the advance to begin.

2. Choose Layout ➤ Typesetting ➤ Advance.

3. Choose a horizontal positioning method.. Your options are None (no horizontal change in position), Left From Insertion Point, Right From Insertion Point, and From Left Edge Of Page.

4. For horizontal positions other than None, specify the Horizontal Distance to advance.

5. Choose a vertical position. Your options are None (no vertical change in position), Up From Insertion Point, Down From Insertion Point, and From Top Of Page.

6. For vertical positions other than None, specify the Vertical Distance to advance.

7. If you chose From Top Of Page, you can select or deselect Text Above Position. This option positions text above (when selected) or below (when deselected) the specified position.

8. Choose OK.

NOTES To return the cursor to the original position, repeat the steps above, but advance in opposite directions by the same distance.

You can't advance text past a page break onto another page, nor can you advance from within a table or columns to above the table or columns.

When using Advance for pre-printed forms, you might find it works best to choose L̲ayout ➤ T̲ypesetting ➤ W̲ord/Letterspac-ing and select B̲aseline Placement For Typesetting. You may also want to enter a fixed line height (L̲ayout ➤ L̲ine ➤ H̲eight ➤ F̲ixed).

 SEE ALSO *Line Height, Typesetting, Units of Measure*

APPEND

The Append command adds selected text or graphics to the existing contents of the Clipboard.

To Add Elements to the Clipboard

1. Select the desired text.

2. Choose E̲dit ➤ Appen̲d.

The Append command is not available unless you've already put something on the Clipboard with E̲dit ➤ C̲opy or E̲dit ➤ Cu̲t. The appended material remains on the Clipboard until you replace it with Cut or Copy or exit Windows.

NOTES All attributes of the appended text, such as bold-face or italics, are preserved when appended to the Clipboard.

SEE ALSO *Combine Documents; Cut, Copy, and Paste; Selecting Text*

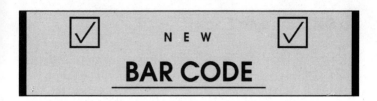

Add POSTNET Bar Codes to mailing addresses to speed up and ensure accurate delivery of your mail.

To Insert a POSTNET Bar Code in a Document

1. Position the cursor where you want the POSTNET Bar Code to appear. Most likely, this will be just above or below the mailing address on a label or envelope.

2. Choose Insert ➤ Other ➤ Bar Code.

3. Enter a 5-digit Zip Code (e.g., 92123), 9-digit Zip+4 Code (e.g., 92123-0987), or 11-digit Delivery Point Bar Code (e.g.,92123-0987-21).

4. Choose OK.

NOTES You can also add POSTNET Bar Codes when defining an envelope via Layout ➤ Envelope. See the Envelope entry.

SEE ALSO *Envelope, Labels, Merge Operations, Paper Size*

BINDING

The Binding command shifts text on the page to provide extra space for binding. Use it if you're planning to bind a document that's printed on both sides of the paper.

To Set a Binding Edge

1. Select Layout ➤ Page ➤ Binding.

2. Choose a binding edge (Left, Right, Top, or Bottom).

3. Specify the Amount of space to leave at the binding edge. To remove the binding offset, enter zero (0).

4. If your printer supports duplexing (printing on both sides of the page), you can choose one of the Duplexing options below:

    Off   No duplexing. (Useful if you don't want duplexing or if your printer can't duplex.)

    From Short Edge   Use when binding on the short side of a page (like a flip chart). This prints text upside down on the back side of a page.

    From Long Edge   Use when binding the long edge of a page (like a book).

5. Choose OK.

NOTES   It's best to set the binding options before you create your document.

A Left binding offset shifts text to the right on odd-numbered pages and to the left on even-numbered pages. A Top binding offset shifts text down on odd-numbered pages and up on even-numbered pages.

The binding offset is added to the inside margin (the margin on the edge that will be bound) and subtracted from the outside margin (the margin on the edge opposite the bound edge).

To get even margins, enter an offset value that's half of what you actually intend and add the same amount to both margins (see Example).

To bind a document that's printed on one side only, choose Layout ➤ Paragraph ➤ Format and specify a Left Margin Adjustment instead of using the Binding feature.

If your printer doesn't support duplex printing, you can print on both sides of the paper by using File ➤ Print ➤ Options ➤ Print Odd/Even Pages. Print odd pages first, then reload the odd pages into the printer to print the even pages on the back side.

EXAMPLE   For a ½-inch binding offset, binding at the left edge, and 1-inch left and right margins, set the binding offset to 0.25 inch and increase the left and right margins to 1.25 inches.

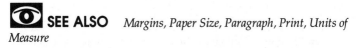 **SEE ALSO**   *Margins, Paper Size, Paragraph, Print, Units of Measure*

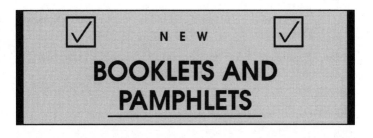

N E W

BOOKLETS AND PAMPHLETS

A booklet typically consists of 8.5×11 (or larger) sheets of paper folded in half and stapled on the fold. A pamphlet is basically the same thing, but folded lengthwise to make a tall, thin, multi-page document that fits in your pocket. This section explains how to set up booklets and pamphlets.

To Set Up a Booklet or Pamphlet

1.   Optionally, choose View ➤ Two Page to view your document.

2.   Move the cursor to the top of the document (press Ctrl+Home twice). Choose Layout ➤ Page ➤ Paper Size, and highlight the paper definition you want. For a standard pamphlet, choose Letter size (8.5×11). For a booklet, choose Letter Landscape (or another landscape definition). If your printer can't print duplex (on both sides), you'll need to choose a definition in Printer Setup that has a paper location of *Manual Feed*. This will let you feed paper manually and print on the back side of the paper. Choose Select.

3.   Choose Layout ➤ Page ➤ Subdivide Page, set Number of Columns to 2, and choose OK.

4.   If you want smaller margins on each page, use Layout ➤ Margins to reduce the margins (for example, to .5 inches all around).

5.   Optionally, add borders around the pages by choosing Layout ➤ Page ➤ Border/Fill. Select a Border Style and choose OK.

6.   Type your document normally. If necessary, insert hard page breaks (Ctrl+↵) to begin new pages.

To Print a Booklet or Pamphlet

1.   If your printer supports duplex printing, move the cursor to the top of the document (press Ctrl+Home), and choose Layout ➤ Page ➤ Binding. Set Duplexing to From Short Edge (for a booklet) or From Long Edge (for a pamphlet). Choose OK.

2.   Choose File ➤ Print ➤ Options, select Booklet Printing, and choose OK.

3.   Choose Print to start printing.

4.   If you chose a paper definition that requires manual feed, insert pages into the printer when prompted. To print on the back (second) side of the paper, feed the paper into the printer blank side up and top edge first (for pamphlets) or left edge first (for booklets). The top or left edge is where headings would appear if you printed them. See your printer's manual if you need more information.

When printing finishes, fold the pages in half and staple them at the fold.

 SEE ALSO   *Binding, Paper Size, Print*

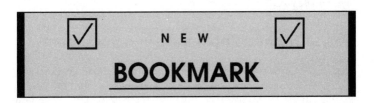

WordPerfect's bookmark feature lets you insert a *bookmark* as a placeholder in text so that you can locate that place again quickly. There are two kinds of bookmarks: QuickMark bookmarks and named bookmarks. Each document can have only one QuickMark bookmark, but as many named bookmarks as you want.

To Create a QuickMark Bookmark

1.   Position the cursor where you want to set the QuickMark.

2.   Press Ctrl+Shift+Q.

To Return the Cursor
to a QuickMark Bookmark

- Press Ctrl+Q.

To Set QuickMarks Automatically

1. Choose File ➤ Preferences and double-click Environment.

2. Select (check) Set QuickMark On Save.

3. Choose OK, then choose Close.

This will automatically set a QuickMark at the cursor position whenever you close any document.

To Use Named Bookmarks in a Document

1. If you want to add a new bookmark or move an existing bookmark, position the cursor where you want the bookmark. If you want to select text at the bookmark when you jump back to it later, select the text now you'll want to jump to later.

2. Choose Insert ➤ Bookmark. You now have several choices:

- To *create a new bookmark,* choose Create, type a unique name for your bookmark, and choose OK. Or, to set a QuickMark bookmark, choose Set QuickMark.

- To *return to an existing bookmark,* highlight its name and choose Go To. To return to a bookmark created with selected text, highlight the bookmark's name and choose Go To & Select. To return to a QuickMark bookmark, choose Find QuickMark.

- To *delete a bookmark,* highlight its name, then choose Delete and answer Yes when prompted. (You can also delete a bookmark by deleting its [Bookmark] code in Reveal Codes.)

- To *move a bookmark* to the current cursor location in your document, highlight the bookmark's name and choose <u>M</u>ove.

- To *rename a bookmark*, highlight the bookmark, choose <u>R</u>ename, edit the name, and choose OK.

3.   Choose <u>C</u>lose, if necessary, to return to the document window.

NOTES   You can get to the Bookmark dialog box quickly by double-clicking any [Bookmark] code in Reveal Codes.

SEE ALSO   *Find, Preferences, Reveal Codes*

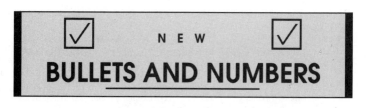

BULLETS AND NUMBERS

The Bullets and Numbers feature lets you type a list in which items are marked automatically with bullets, numbers, roman numerals, or letters.

To Type a Bulleted or Numbered List

1.   Position the cursor where you want the list to begin.

2.   Choose <u>I</u>nsert ➤ Bullets & <u>N</u>umbers

12   Bullets and Numbers

3. In the Styles list, highlight the character you want to put at the start of the item. (If you choose a number, roman numeral, or letter, WordPerfect will increment markers automatically when you add a list item and will decrement markers when you delete an item.)

4. If you want a new bullet or number to appear automatically when you press ↵, select New Bullet Or Number On ENTER.

5. If necessary, select Starting Value and enter a starting number for the first marked item.

6. Choose OK.

7. Type the text of the item and press ↵. (If you didn't select New Bullet Or Number On ENTER in step 4, you can add a blank line by pressing ↵ a second time.)

To type the remaining items in the list, use either of the methods below:

- If you selected New Bullet Or Number on ENTER in step 4 above, type the next item and press ↵. Repeat this step until you've typed all the items. When you're done, choose Insert ➤ Bullets & Numbers, select <None> in the Styles list, and choose OK.

- If you didn't select New Bullet Or Number On ENTER in step 4, press Ctrl+Shift+B, type the next item, and press ↵ (twice if you want a blank line between items). Repeat this step until you've typed all the items.

NOTES   To change the style of bulleted or numbered items in a list created with this feature, choose Insert ➤ Bullets & Numbers. Highlight the style you want to change and choose Edit. Edit the style as you would any style, then choose OK twice.

If you selected New Bullet Or Number On ENTER in step 4 and want to add blank lines between items, position the cursor just above the list, or select all the items in the list. Choose Layout ➤ Paragraph ➤ Format ➤ Spacing Between Paragraghs, enter a Spacing greater than 1, and choose OK. For example, a line spacing of 2 puts one blank line between entries.

 SEE ALSO   *Line Spacing, List, Outline, Styles*

BUTTON BAR

The button bars provide shortcut buttons for many WordPerfect operations. WordPerfect comes with twelve predefined button bars. You can customize any button bar and create new ones. To find out what a button does, move the mouse pointer to the button and read the description in the title bar at the top of the screen.

To Display or Hide the Button Bar

- Choose View ➤ Button Bar, or click the View Button Bar button in the power bar.

You can also hide the button bar by right-clicking it and choosing Hide Button Bar.

To Select a Button Bar

1. Display the button if it isn't visible (View ➤ Button Bar).

2. Right-click the button bar and choose the button bar you want from the QuickMenu.

You can also select a button bar by choosing File ➤ Preferences and double-clicking Button Bar. Highlight the button bar you want and choose Select, then Close.

To Reposition the Button Bar

1. Display the button bar if it isn't visible.

2. Move the mouse pointer to a blank area on the button bar (the pointer changes to a hand icon).

3. Drag the button bar to where you want it. If you drag the bar somewhere other than the edge of the screen, it becomes a window that you can move and size.

To Change the Appearance of the Button Bar

1. Display the button bar if it isn't visible.

2. Right-click the button bar and choose Preferences from the QuickMenu.

3. Choose Options.

4. Select the Font Face, Font Size, Appearance (Text, Picture, or Picture And Text), and screen Location (Left, Top, Right, Bottom, or Palette) for the button bar.

5. Choose OK, then Close.

NOTES   You can add, delete, and move buttons on a button bar; create new button bars; and delete existing button bars. To get started with these operations, right-click the button bar and choose Preferences. Or choose File ➤ Preferences and double-click the Button Bar icon. See the Preferences entry for more information.

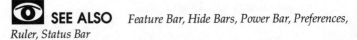 **SEE ALSO**   *Feature Bar, Hide Bars, Power Bar, Preferences, Ruler, Status Bar*

CANCEL

Cancel is WordPerfect's universal "get me out of trouble" feature. Use it to back out of menu choices, cancel any operation that displays a prompt or menu, or stop a macro or merge operation before it finishes.

To Cancel the Current Operation

Cancel an operation in any of the following ways:

- Choose Cancel from a dialog box.

- Double-click the Control-menu box of a dialog box you want to back out of.

- Click the document window outside an open menu you want to cancel.

- Using the keyboard, press Escape (Esc).

NOTES   You may need to cancel more than once when backing out of menus to reach the document window.

SEE ALSO   *Document Window, Exit, Undelete, Undo*

CENTER

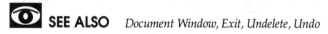

You can center text horizontally between margins or within columns.

To Center One Line of Text

1. Position the cursor where you want to center new text or at the beginning of an existing line of text.

2. Choose Layout ➤ Line ➤ Center (Shift+F7). WordPerfect will center the text between the margins.

3. If you want dot leaders, repeat step 2.

4. If you are centering new text, type the new text and press ↵.

To Center Large Sections of Text

1. Position the cursor above the text to be centered, or select a block of text.

2. Choose Layout ➤ Justification ➤ Center, or press Ctrl+E.

The text will be centered horizontally until the next justification code or until the end of the document.

NOTES To center text vertically (top to bottom) on the page, see Center Page.

SEE ALSO *Center Page, Justification, Page Breaks, Selecting Text, Tabs*

CENTER PAGE

This command centers all text vertically on the page between the top and bottom margins.

To Center Text Vertically

1. Position the cursor at the top of the page of text to be centered.

2. Choose Layout ➤ Page ➤ Center.

3. Choose a centering option (Current Page, Current And Subsequent Pages, or No Centering).

4. Choose OK.

 NOTES   If additional text follows the text to be centered vertically (for example, a document that follows a centered title page), move the cursor to the end of the vertically centered text and insert a hard page break (Ctrl+↵).

SEE ALSO   *Center, Page Breaks*

CHARACTERS

WordPerfect lets you enter hundreds of characters that you can't otherwise type on your keyboard. These include mathematical, scientific, multinational, typographic, and iconic symbols, as well as letters for several foreign-language alphabets.

To Insert a Special Character

1.   Position the cursor where you want the special character to appear.

2.   Press Ctrl+W or choose Insert ➤ Character.

3.   Do either of the following:

  • Choose a character set from the Character Set pop-up list button, then click on the character you want in the Characters list.

  • Choose Number and type the character set number, a comma, and the character number. For example, choose Number and type **5,0** for the heart character in the Iconic Symbols character set.

4.   To insert the character and return to your document, choose Insert And Close. To insert the character and remain in the WordPerfect Characters dialog box, choose Insert. (If you choose Insert, you can repeat steps 3–4 as needed; then choose Close to return to the document window.)

 SEE ALSO   *Font, Overstrike*

N E W

CHART

WordPerfect has a built-in charting package that can produce pie, bar, line, area, scatter, and hi-lo charts in many different formats. You can enter data into the Chart application's data table, or you can chart data that's stored in a table in your document. Finished charts are placed into graphics boxes in your document.

Chart 19

To Create a Chart

1. If you want to chart a table that's in your document, position the cursor anywhere in the table.

2. Choose <u>G</u>raphics ➤ Cha<u>r</u>t, or click the Chart button in the WordPerfect button bar. The Chart Editor will open, as shown in Figure 1.

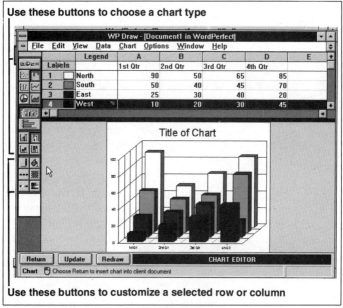

Use these buttons to choose a chart type

Use these buttons to customize a selected row or column

Figure 1: The WordPerfect Chart Editor

3. If necessary, update the data in the data table in the top half of the window. The basic techniques are the same as for changing tables. You can also use these techniques:

- To *clear all the data* in the table, choose <u>F</u>ile ➤ C<u>l</u>ear or press Ctrl+Shift+F4, then choose <u>Y</u>es.

- To *select (highlight) columns or rows* in the table, click on the label for the column or row, or drag the mouse through the column or row labels to select several at once. (You can also hold down the Shift key and press an arrow key to select columns, rows, or cells.)

- To *insert and delete columns or rows* in the table, select the column or row. Then choose Edit ➤ Insert or Edit ➤ Delete, as appropriate.

- To *cut or copy and paste* data, position the cursor in a cell or select cells, rows, or columns. Choose Edit then Cut or Copy. Position the cursor where you want to paste the data. Choose Edit, then Paste or Paste Transposed. (Paste Transposed converts row data to column data and vice versa.)

- To *go to a specific cell,* choose Edit ➤ Go To Cell or press Ctrl+G, specify the cell address, and choose OK.

4. Use any of the techniques below to customize the appearance of the chart:

- To *choose a chart type,* click a chart button in the Chart palette (see Figure 1). Or, choose options from the Chart menu.

- To *customize a data series,* select the row(s) or column(s) you want to change. Then click on the Turn Object Outline On/Off, Turn Object Fill On/Off, Set Line Styles, Set Fill Pattern Style, Set Line Color, or Set Fill Color buttons as needed. Or, choose Options ➤ Series and choose options from the Series Options dialog box.

- To *redraw the chart,* click the Redraw button in the Chart editor, press Ctrl+F3, or choose View ➤ Redraw.

- To *update the chart* in the document window, click the Update button in the Chart editor, or choose File ➤ Update Document.

- To *display or hide the Default Chart button bar,* choose View ➤ Button Bar or press F10.

- To *control the data table* appearance or to include or exclude a row or column from the chart, choose options from the Data menu.

- To *customize the chart's layout,* series axes, grid and tick marks, frame, perspective, titles, legend, or labels, choose options from the Options menu.

Chart 21

- To *change labels for the legend,* type the labels in the Legend column of the data table, in the row for whatever series the label describes.

- To *get help with charting,* choose options from the Help menu.

5. To return to the document window and insert (or update) the chart, click the Return button in the Chart editor, or choose File ➤ Exit And Return To Document. If prompted, choose Yes to save your changes.

To Edit an Existing Chart

- In the document window, double-click the chart's graphics box.

- Or right-click the box and choose WP Chart 2.1 Object ➤ Edit from the QuickMenu.

To Annotate a Chart in the Draw Package

- In the document window, right-click the chart box and choose WP Chart 2.1 Object ➤ Annotate from the QuickMenu.

NOTES   The easiest way to learn the Chart package is to use the guidelines given above and then experiment.

You can move the mouse pointer to most buttons in the Chart palette to find out what the buttons are for. A description of the button will appear in the title bar of the window.

Once created, a chart box can be sized, captioned, positioned, and edited in the same way as any normal graphics box.

SEE ALSO   *Draw, Graphics and Graphics Boxes, Spreadsheet/Database Import and Link, Tables*

CODES

Codes are used to control formatting in WordPerfect. Normally these are hidden, unless you turn on the Reveal Codes screen (View ➤ Reveal Codes or Alt+F3). See the Reveal Codes command reference for details about using the Reveal Codes screen.

NOTES   *Single codes* affect all text beyond them, up to another single code that changes the setting. *Paired codes* affect individual blocks of text.

In the example below, [Ln Spacing:2.00] is a single code that double-spaces all text below it (up to the next [Ln Spacing] code, if any). The [Italc] codes are paired codes that italicize the *Getting Started* text between the codes.

[Ln Spacing:2.0][Italc]Getting Started[Italc]: To start the engine, insert the key and turn it to the right

Codes are inserted automatically when you press a formatting key (such as Tab or ↵), or when you choose formatting options from the menus. To find out what a code is for, turn on Reveal Codes (Alt+F3) and point to the code with your mouse. A description of the code will appear in the WordPerfect title bar.

You can find and replace *specific codes* (such as a certain font) or *general codes* (such as any type of Tab).

SEE ALSO   *Find, Initial Codes Style, Initial Font, Replace, Reveal Codes, Styles*

COLUMNS

The Columns command lets you format text and graphics into multiple columns.

To Define Columns

1. Move the cursor to where the columns should begin.

2. Choose Layout ➤ Columns ➤ Define, double-click the Columns Define button in the power bar, or right-click the ruler bar and choose Columns.

3. Choose Columns and specify the number of columns you want (between 2 and 24, inclusive).

4. Choose one of the following types of columns:

    Newspaper   "Snaking" columns, in which text ends at the bottom of one column and resumes at the top of the next.

    Balanced Newspaper   "Snaking" text is equally distributed between columns.

    Parallel   Each column is printed independently, side-by-side on a page; each column's text carries over to the next page.

    Parallel w/Block Protect   This format is the same as parallel, except that the full block of side-by-side columns stays together, and the whole block moves to the next page if one column spills over.

5. If you wish, you can customize the spacing between columns, the line spacing between rows in parallel columns, and the widths of individual columns. The sample page in the Columns dialog box will reflect each change you make.

6. Choose OK.

WordPerfect inserts a [Col Def] code at the cursor position and turns the columns on.

To Define Columns
with the Power Bar and Ruler Bar

1. If they aren't visible, turn on the power bar (<u>V</u>iew ➤ P<u>o</u>wer Bar) and ruler bar (<u>V</u>iew ➤ <u>R</u>uler Bar).

2. Use the Columns Define button in the power bar to define the number of columns you want.

3. If you want to adjust the column spacing, drag the column margin markers on the ruler bar to the desired position.

To Turn Columns On or Off

1. Position the cursor where you want to turn columns on or off. (The cursor must be to the right of the [Col Def] code that defines the columns.)

2. To turn columns off, choose <u>L</u>ayout ➤ <u>C</u>olumns ➤ <u>O</u>ff. To turn columns on, choose <u>L</u>ayout ➤ <u>C</u>olumns ➤ <u>D</u>efine ➤ OK.

To Edit Text in Columns

Use standard editing and cursor positioning techniques, with these exceptions:

- To *start a new column*, press Ctrl+↵, or choose <u>L</u>ayout ➤ <u>C</u>olumns ➤ <u>C</u>olumn Break. Newspaper and balanced newspaper columns are started automatically, but you can start a new column earlier by inserting a column break. In parallel columns (or parallel columns with block protect), inserting a column break moves text to the next column.

- To *move the cursor from column to column* without inserting text, use your mouse, or press Alt+← or Alt+→.

- To *move the cursor to the top or bottom* of the current column, press Alt+Home or Alt+End, respectively.

To Change the Number of Columns

Use either of the techniques below:

- To *change the number of columns,* position the cursor where you want the new number of columns to take effect. Then follow the steps above for defining columns and specify a different number of columns.

- To *delete the columnar format entirely,* turn on Reveal Codes (Alt+F3) and delete the column definition code [Col Def] and its associated hard page break codes [HPg].

NOTES You can set a columnar format before or after you've entered text and graphics.

You can't define columns within footnotes, endnotes, or tables.

SEE ALSO *Cursor, Power Bar, Reveal Codes, Ruler, Tables, Units of Measure*

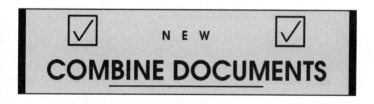

COMBINE DOCUMENTS

You can combine WordPerfect documents by inserting another file anywhere within the current document.

To Insert a File into the Current Document

1. Position the cursor where you want to add the file.

2. Choose Insert ➤ File.

3. Type in the name of the desired file or highlight the name you want, then click Insert.

4. Choose <u>Y</u>es when asked "Insert file into current document?"

 NOTES <u>F</u>ile ➤ <u>O</u>pen opens a file in a new window.

 SEE ALSO *File Management, Open*

COMMENT

You can use the Comment feature to add nonprinting comments to a document or to convert existing comments to text.

To Add a Comment to a Document

1. Move the cursor to where you want the comment to appear.

2. Choose <u>I</u>nsert ➤ Co<u>m</u>ment ➤ <u>C</u>reate. Or, right-click in the far left margin and choose <u>C</u>omment from the Quick-Menu. A comment editing window and feature bar will appear.

3. Type your comment as you would any text. You can also use the optional buttons in the Comment feature bar to insert your <u>I</u>nitials or Na<u>m</u>e (see "To Customize Document Comments," below) and the system <u>D</u>ate or <u>T</u>ime.

4. If you want to edit the next or previous comment in the document, click the <u>N</u>ext or <u>P</u>revious buttons in the Comment feature bar.

5. When you're done typing the comment, click the <u>C</u>lose button in the Comment feature bar.

In Draft view, a shaded comment box will appear in your document and the comment text will be visible.

In Page or Two-Page view, a comment icon will appear in the left margin of the document window. You'll need to click the comment icon to see the comment text. (To hide the comment again, click anywhere in the document window).

To Change a Document Comment

Use any of the methods below to reach the comment editing window:

- Double-click the comment box or icon.

- Turn on Reveal Codes (Alt+F3) and double-click the [Comment] code.

- Move the cursor to just after the comment you want to change, then choose Insert ➤ Comment ➤ Edit.

- Right-click the comment icon or box and choose Edit.

Make whatever changes you wish, then click the Close button in the Comment feature bar.

To Delete Comments

- To *delete one comment*, turn on Reveal Codes (Alt+F3) and delete the appropriate comment code [Comment]. Or, right-click the comment icon or box you want to delete, then choose Delete from the QuickMenu.

- To *delete all comments* in one step, press Ctrl+Home twice, then choose Edit ➤ Replace (Ctrl+F2), choose Match ➤ Codes, double-click *Comment* in the Find Codes list, choose Replace All, then choose Close.

To Convert Text to a Comment

1. Select the text that you want to convert to a comment.

2. Choose Insert ➤ Comment ➤ Create. Or, right-click in the far left margin and choose Comment from the QuickMenu.

To Convert a Comment to Text

1.   Move the cursor just beyond the comment you want to convert to text.

2.   Choose Insert ➤ Comment ➤ Convert to Text.

3.   If necessary, add spaces or hard returns (↵) to blend the newly converted text with existing text.

To Hide or Display Document Comments

1.   Choose File ➤ Preferences and double-click Display.

2.   To hide comments, clear the Comments check box. To display comments, check the Comments box.

3.   Choose OK, then choose Close.

To Customize Document Comments

1.   Choose File ➤ Preferences and double-click Environment.

2.   In the User Info… area of the Environment Preferences dialog box, do any of the following:

   • Choose Name, then type the name you want inserted when you click the Name button in the Comment feature bar.

   • Choose Initials, then type the initials you want to appear in the comment icon and when you click the Initials button.

   • Click the User Color button, then click the color you want to use as the background whenever you add a new comment.

3.   Choose OK, then choose Close.

Your changes will affect new comments that you create (existing comments will be unaffected).

 SEE ALSO *Delete, Document Window, Feature Bar, Reveal Codes, Selecting Text, View*

CONVERT CASE

This command converts selected text to UPPERCASE, lowercase, or Initial Cap Letters.

To Convert the Case of Selected Text

1. Select the text that you want to convert.

2. Choose Edit ➤ Convert Case.

3. Choose either Lowercase, Uppercase, or Initial Capitals.

SEE ALSO *Selecting Text*

COUNTER

You can use Counters to count or number anything in your document, including paragraphs, chapters, sections, graphic boxes, widget names—whatever! WordPerfect has built-in system counters for the five types of graphic boxes. These counters are updated and displayed in captions automatically. However, you must manually increment, decrement, and display counters that you create.

To Create a Counter

1.   Position the cursor where you want to create a counter.

2.   Choose Insert ➤ Other ➤ Counter ➤ Create.

3.   In the Counter Name box, type a name for the counter.

4.   Specify the number of Levels (up to 5) and the Numbering Method for each level.

5.   Choose OK, then choose Close.

To Change or Display a Counter

1.   Position the cursor where you want the counter to change.

2.   Choose Insert ➤ Other ➤ Counter and highlight the counter you want to change or display.

3.   Choose any of the following options as needed:

Edit   Lets you change the highlighted counter's name, number of levels, and numbering method.

Delete   Deletes the highlighted counter. You can only delete the counter itself, not an individual level. (Use Edit to reduce the number of levels in a counter.) You can't delete a built-in system counter.

Value   Lets you set each level of the highlighted counter to a specific value.

Increase   Increases the highlighted counter's value by 1.

Decrease   Decreases the highlighted counter's value by 1.

Display In Document   Displays the highlighted counter's value at the cursor position.

Increase and Display Increases the highlighted counter's value by 1 and displays it in your document.

Decrease and Display Decreases the highlighted counter's value by 1 and displays it in your document.

4. If necessary, choose C̲lose.

👁 **SEE ALSO** *Cross-Reference, Graphics and Graphics Boxes, Line Numbering, Lists, Outline, Page Numbering*

CROSS-REFERENCE

You can use WordPerfect's automatic cross-referencing features to reference page numbers, paragraph or outline numbers, footnote and endnote numbers, and graphics box numbers.

References tell the reader to look somewhere else, as in "see Figure 5.3" or "see Footnote 4." A *target* is the place (such as a page number, figure, or table) where you're sending the reader.

Generate cross-references involves two processes:

- Set up the targets and references. You need to mark a target only once, then you can mark as many references to that target as you need. (You can define targets before references, or references before targets. However, the instructions below assume you're defining the targets first.)

- Generate the cross-references. (Choose T̲ools ➤ Ge̲nerate, click the G̲enerate button on the Cross-Reference feature bar, or press Ctrl+F9. Then choose OK.)

To Mark a Target

1.   Choose Tools ➤ Cross-Reference to display the Cross-Reference feature bar.

2.   Move the cursor just past the target. If necessary, use Reveal Codes (Alt+F3) to help you position the cursor. (When marking a page number target for a footnote or endnote, the cursor must be in the footnote or endnote.)

3.   From the Reference drop-down list button in the feature bar, select the type of item you're targeting. Your options are Page, Secondary Page, Chapter, Volume, Paragraph/Outline, Footnote, Endnote, Caption Number (for graphics boxes), and Counter.

4.   In the feature bar's Target text box, type a descriptive name for the target.

5.   Click the Mark Target button in the feature bar.

To Mark a Reference

1.   Choose Tools ➤ Cross-Reference to display the Cross-Reference feature bar.

2.   Place the cursor where you want the reference to appear.

3.   Type any introductory text and then enter a blank space, if necessary. For example, type **[see page** and then press the spacebar.

4.   In the feature bar's Target text box, type the target name (exactly as you specified it when marking the target), or select the target name from the Target drop-down list.

5.   Click the Mark Reference button in the feature bar. (The question mark (?) in the reference will be replaced by the correct reference when you generate the lists and references.)

6. Finish typing any introductory text for the reference. For instance, type a space and then] to finish the example started in step 3.

NOTES You don't have to include text from the caption number style in your introductory text. WordPerfect will automatically insert text from the caption number style of any graphics box when it generates references. For instance, if you mark Figure 1 as a target, WordPerfect will insert the words *Figure 1* in the reference automatically.

You must generate cross-references again if you make changes that affect the numbering of targets.

You can create cross-references for an individual document or for a master document (see the Master Document entry).

To delete a cross reference or target, turn on Reveal Codes (Alt+F3) and delete the appropriate [Ref] or [Target] code.

You can combine cross-references, as in the examples below:

- References to multiple targets of different types (e.g., *see page 1, Figure 2*). For this example, you'd define a Page target and Caption Number target, then create the references to each target as described above.

- References to multiple targets with the same reference type (e.g., *see pages 10, 12, 14*). For this example, you'd define three Page targets. Then create the references to each target as described above.

- Page *x* of *y* references in headers and footers. For this example, create a Page target on the last page (name it **Last Page**). Then create a header or footer, type **Page** and a space, and use the Number button in the Header/Footer feature bar to insert the page number. Type **of** and a space, then insert a reference to the **Last Page** target.

SEE ALSO   *Counter; Footnotes and Endnotes; Generate; Graphics and Graphics Boxes; Headers, Footers, and Watermarks; Lists; Master Document; Outline; Page Numbering; Tables*

CURSOR

The *cursor* shows where the next character that you type will appear in the document window or in Reveal Codes. On the document window, the cursor is usually a small, blinking vertical bar. In Reveal Codes, the cursor is a solid block. You can position the cursor with the mouse or the keyboard (whichever is easiest for you).

To Move the Cursor with the Mouse

- Position the mouse pointer just before the character (or code) and click the left mouse button. (If the character or code isn't visible, use the scroll bar to bring it into view.)

The mouse pointer usually appears as an I-beam on the document window. In Reveal Codes, it appears as an I-beam when pointing to text and as an arrow when pointing to a code.

To Move the Cursor with the Keyboard

- Press a cursor movement key or key combination (e.g., arrow keys, Home, End, Ctrl+→, Ctrl+←). For most operations, you can press the positioning keys shown in Table I.

Table I: Keyboard Methods for Moving the Cursor (Most
Operations)

TO MOVE TO	PRESS
Beginning of document (after any codes)	Ctrl+Home
Beginning of document (before any codes)	Ctrl+Home,Ctrl+Home
Beginning of line (after any codes)	Home
Bottom of screen (then down one screen at a time)	PgDn
Down one line	↓
Down one paragraph	Ctrl+↓
End of document (after any codes)	Ctrl+End
End of line (after any codes)	End
Far left end of line (before any codes)	Home,Home
First line on previous page	Alt+PgUp
First line on next page	Alt+PgDn
Left one character	←
Left one word	Ctrl+←
Right one character	→
Right one word	Ctrl+→
Top of screen (then up one screen at a time)	PgUp
Up one line	↑
Up one paragraph	Ctrl+↑

NOTES   You must position the cursor before adding, changing, deleting, or moving text and most formatting codes. You can either type over or insert characters at the cursor.

You can't move the cursor beyond the last character or code in a document or before the first code.

If the cursor doesn't seem to move when you're at the document window, it may be resting on a hidden code. Continue moving the cursor past the code, or turn on Reveal Codes (Alt+F3) to make the code visible.

To customize the behavior of the cursor when it moves through hidden codes, choose File ➤ Preferences and double-click Environment. Then select or deselect Confirm Deletion Of Codes, Stop Insertion Point At Hidden Codes. Choose OK and Close.

SEE ALSO   *Codes, Document Window, Go To, Insert/Type-over, Mouse, Reveal Codes*

CUT, COPY, AND PASTE

Use cut, copy, and paste to move or copy selected data within and between documents, including those in other Windows applications. Copying leaves the original data intact. Cutting removes it from the original position.

To Cut, Copy, and Paste Data

1.   Select the data you want to cut or copy.

2.   Choose Edit ➤ Cut (Ctrl+X or Shift+Del), or Edit ➤ Copy (Ctrl+C or Ctrl+Ins). Or right-click the selected data and choose Cut or Copy from the QuickMenu. (If the Clipboard

already contains some data, you can add the selected data
to the end of the Clipboard by choosing Edit ➤ Append.)

3. Move the cursor to where you want the data to appear.
If it's another WordPerfect document, open that document and position the cursor. If it's another application,
open the application and file and position the cursor.

4. Use any of the following methods to paste the data at the
cursor position:

- In a WordPerfect document, choose Edit ➤ Paste
(Ctrl+V or Shift+Ins), or right-click and select Paste
from the QuickMenu.

- In another application, you can choose Edit ➤ Paste
(Ctrl+V or Shift+Ins). Or, if the application supports object linking and embedding, you can choose Edit ➤
Paste Link or Edit ➤ Paste Special. (See the Object Linking and Embedding Entry and your application's documentation for details.)

NOTES The Windows Clipboard maintains its data until
you cut or copy more data or exit Windows. You can paste from the
Clipboard to as many locations as you want.

See your Windows documentation to find out how to view what's
on the Clipboard.

SEE ALSO *Append, Drag and Drop, Object Linking and
Embedding, Selecting Text, Undo*

DATE/TIME

The Date/Time command allows you to insert the current date and/or time as either code or text.

To Set the Date/Time Format

1.   Choose Insert ➤ Date ➤ Date Format.

2.   Highlight a format from the list of Predefined Formats, and optionally customize that format using the Custom button.

3.   Choose OK to return.

These settings affect only dates that you add to the current document beyond the current cursor position.

To Insert the Date/ Time in a Document

1.   Move the cursor to where you want the date to appear, then choose Insert ➤ Date.

2.   Choose either Date Text (Ctrl+D) or Date Code (Ctrl+Shift+D), depending on which you want to insert.

Alternatively, you can press Ctrl+D to insert date text, or Ctrl+Shift+D to insert the date code.

NOTES   If you enter a code, it will automatically be updated to reflect the current system date whenever you retrieve or print the document. Dates entered as text will *not* be updated. The system date and time are determined by the DOS commands DATE and TIME, and the Date/Time applet in the Windows Control Panel.

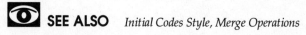 **SEE ALSO**   *Initial Codes Style, Merge Operations*

DECIMAL ALIGNMENT

The decimal align character (initially ".") is used to vertically align tabbed text or text in tables, and the thousands separator (initially ",") is used to align numbers in math calculations.

To Change the Alignment Character

1. Move the cursor to above the first number you want to realign.

2. Choose Layout ➤ Line ➤ Tab Set.

3. In the Character text box under Align Character, delete the existing character and type the character that you want the numbers to align on or press Ctrl+W and select a character from the WordPerfect Characters dialog box. Then choose OK.

Only decimal-aligned text that's below the cursor position and contains the character you specified in step 3 will be aligned on that character.

To Change the Thousands Separator

1. Move the cursor to above the first number you want to realign.

2. Choose Layout ➤ Line ➤ Other Codes ➤ Thousands Separator.

3. In the Thousands Separator text box, type the character that you want to use as a thousands separator, or press Ctrl+W and select a character from the WordPerfect Characters dialog box.

4. Choose Insert.

 SEE ALSO *Tables*, *Tabs*

DELAY CODES

This feature lets you insert page formatting codes that won't take effect until a certain page. For example, you can define page formatting codes for headers, footers, or page numbers at the top of a document, but delay the execution of those codes until a certain page (i.e., after the title page, Table of Contents, and so forth).

To Delay Formatting Codes

1. Move the cursor to the top of the document, or to any location before the page where you want formatting to take effect.

2. Choose Layout ➤ Page ➤ Delay Codes.

3. Specify the number of pages (from the current page) to delay the new codes, and choose OK.

4. A Define Delayed Codes editing window and feature bar will appear. Create the features you want to delay just as you normally would when editing a document. Or, use the feature bar buttons to specify a Paper Size or create a Figure, Header/Footer, or Watermark. Each time you finish setting up a feature, WordPerfect will add that feature's code to the Define Delayed Codes editing window.

5. When you're done entering codes to delay, choose the Close button in the feature bar.

To Change a Delay Code

To edit a Delay code(s) feature, double-click the [Delay] code you want to change and make modifications as necessary. When you are done, choose the Close button on the feature bar.

NOTES Only open codes and graphics can be delayed. Paired codes and some codes used in formatting such as Indent, Center, Flush Right, and Tab cannot be delayed.

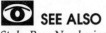 **SEE ALSO**   *Headers, Footers, and Watermarks; Initial Codes Style; Page Numbering*

DELETE

Use this command to delete anything in your document. If you make a mistake, you can instantly undelete it.

To Delete Text and Codes

Use any method below:

- Press Delete (Del) to delete the character (or code) to the right of the cursor.

- Press Backspace to delete the character (or code) to the left of the cursor.

- Select the text (or codes) you want to delete, then press Delete (Del) or Backspace.

- Use one of the following shortcut keys:

Ctrl+Backspace	Delete word
Ctrl+Del	Delete to end of line
Ctrl+Shift+Del	Delete to end of page

To Delete a Code from Reveal Codes

- Move the mouse pointer to the code you want to delete, then drag the code off of the Reveal Codes screen (up into the document window).

To Delete a Table

1. Move the mouse pointer to one of the lines inside the table, until it becomes a vertical or horizontal arrow (not the usual angled arrow).

2. Triple-click the mouse button to select all the cells in the table.

3. Press Delete (Del), choose Entire Table, then choose OK.

To Delete a Graphics Box

- Click the graphics box once to select it, then press Delete (Del).

- Or drag the hidden code for the graphics box off of the Reveal Codes screen.

To Undelete

1. If necessary, move the cursor back to the place where you made the accidental deletion.

2. Choose Edit ➤ Undelete, or press Ctrl+Shift+Z.

3. Choose Restore. (See Undelete for more information.)

To Delete a File

1. First, make sure that the file you want to delete isn't open in any applications. (Close the file if it's open in WordPerfect.)

2. Choose File ➤ Open (Ctrl+O).

3. Highlight the name of the file you want to delete, then choose File Options ➤ Delete or press Del.

4. Choose Delete again at the prompt.

5. Choose Cancel in the Open File dialog box to return to your document.

You cannot use WordPerfect's Undelete to undelete a file. Instead, you'll need to use the DOS UNDELETE command, File ➤ Undelete in the Windows File Manager (if available), or a third-party utility program.

 NOTES   To delete a code or item of text throughout the document, use the Edit ➤ Replace (Ctrl+F2) commands to replace the text/codes you want to delete with "nothing."

Deleting one code of a paired code (e.g., [Bold] or [Italc]) automatically deletes the other code.

SEE ALSO   *Replace, Selecting Text, Undelete, Undo*

DIALOG BOXES

A dialog box appears whenever you choose a menu option that requires additional information.

To Make Selections in a Dialog Box

The current default option within a dialog box is outlined with a dashed line or highlighted. You can use any of the following methods to choose an option:

- Click on the option you want.

- Press Tab (to move forward) or Shift+Tab (to move backward) to highlight or outline the item you want. Then click the option or press the spacebar to select it.

- If the option you want has an underlined letter, you can choose the option by holding down Alt and typing that letter. (If necessary, click the option, press ALT+↓, or press the spacebar to open the options menu or dialog box.)

- If the option is a toggle (like a check box), use the spacebar to turn it on and off.

To Save/Abandon Dialog Box Selections

If you want to save and activate your selections in a dialog box, choose Close or OK. If you want to abandon the current dialog box without saving any selections, choose the Cancel button or press Esc.

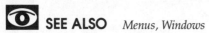 **NOTES** All Windows applications use dialog boxes with similar controls. To learn more about dialog boxes, please refer to your Windows documentation.

SEE ALSO *Menus, Windows*

DOCUMENT COMPARE

This feature compares the document on the screen to another document on disk (presumably an earlier version of the same document). WordPerfect marks phrases in the current document that differ from the stored version.

To Compare Two Documents

1. Open one of the documents that you want to compare and choose File ➤ Compare Document ➤ Add Markings.

2. Enter the name, and, if necessary, the path of the document on disk that you want to compare to your current document. Or, click on the File button and select a different path and file name.

3. Choose the Word, Phrase, Sentence, or Paragraph option button, depending on how you want to compare the two documents.

4. Choose OK.

Redline and strikeout codes are inserted to surround the changed phrases. Deleted phrases appear with a line drawn through the text. Added phrases appear in red if you have a color monitor. Moved phrases are surrounded by notices.

To Remove Marks from a Document

- Choose File ➤ Compare Document ➤ Remove Markings, select Remove Redline Markings and Strikeout Text or Remove Strikeout Text Only, and click OK.

- Or, choose Edit ➤ Undo (Ctrl+Z) immediately after you compare the documents.

 SEE ALSO   *Font*

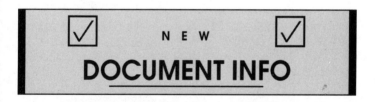

N E W

DOCUMENT INFO

Document Info displays statistics about the current document.

To Display Document Statistics

1. Choose File ➤ Document Info.

2. After reviewing the results, choose OK.

DOCUMENTS/BACKUP

Documents/Backup can automatically back up files in two ways: by saving documents at timed intervals and by saving a copy of the original file each time you replace it with a newer version.

To Control Timed and Original Backups

1.   Select File ➤ Preferences and double-click File.

2.   Select from the the following options:

Default Directory	Accept the default or make changes as you desire.
Timed Document Backup Every *n* Minutes	Make timed backups. You must enter the number of minutes between saves; 10 minutes is the default.
Backup Directory	Specify the directory where you want timed backups to appear. If you leave this option blank, timed backups will be stored in the same directory as your WIN.COM program (usually C:\WINDOWS).
Original Document Backup	Back up the original file.

3.   Choose OK, then choose Close.

NOTES   If the timed backup files exist the next time you start WordPerfect, you'll be asked to rename, open, or delete them before being taken to the document window. If you open them, you can recover all your work up to the moment of interruption. If you delete them, they are lost forever. Timed backups are named WP{WP}.BK*n*, where *n* is the document number of the backup file.

Original backups are always stored in the same directory as your document file. The old version of the original file is named <file-name>.BK! and will remain on disk after you exit WordPerfect.

When you recover an original backup file, rename it immediately to remove the .BK! extension.

 SEE ALSO   *Preferences, Save/Save As*

DOCUMENT SUMMARY

Document summary allows you to create summary information about a document. Use this information to help you locate and identify documents in the future.

To Create or Edit a Summary

1. Choose File ➤ Document Summary.

2. Fill in any descriptive text you want. Optionally, you can use the Configure button to choose other fields to display in the summary. You can also choose between Options to print, save, extract or delete the summary information.

3. Choose OK.

 SEE ALSO   *Print*

DOCUMENT WINDOW

The document window is where most editing operations take place. The *cursor* (also called the *insertion point)* indicates where the next character that you type will appear.

To Open a Document Window

- To start a new document in an empty document window, choose File ➤ New (Ctrl+n or Shift+F4).

- To open an existing document in its own window, choose File ➤ Open (Ctrl+O).

 NOTES You can have up to nine document windows on-screen at a time, but only one can be active. The active document window will be in the foreground with its title bar darkened. To switch from one window to another, click on the title bar or choose the document window name from the Window menu. Or, press Ctrl+F6 to switch to the next document and Ctrl+Shift+F6 to switch to the previous document.

Use the standard Windows techniques to maximize, minimize, size, and move the document window (see your Windows manual if you need help.) Choose Window ➤ Cascade or Window ➤ Tile to rearrange the document windows on your screen.

Shift+F4 opens a new, cascaded document window on the display.

SEE ALSO *File Management, New, Open, Reveal Codes*

DRAG AND DROP

This command lets you move and copy text using the mouse instead of menus or shortcut keys.

To Drag and Drop Text

1. Select the text you want to move or copy.

2. Move the pointer to the selected text and hold down the mouse button. A small icon appears on the pointer.

3. If you want to copy rather than move the text, hold down the Ctrl key.

4. Drag the mouse pointer to the new location for the text. You can scroll off any edge of the screen to keep moving in that direction.

5. When the mouse pointer gets to the destination for the moved or copied text, release the mouse button. If you copied text, release the Ctrl key *after* releasing the mouse button.

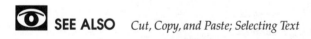 **SEE ALSO**   *Cut, Copy, and Paste; Selecting Text*

DRAW

You can use Draw to create a new drawing or to modify an existing image.

To Start Draw

- To create a new drawing from scratch, choose Graphics ➤ Draw or click the Draw button on the WordPerfect button bar.

- To edit an existing image with Draw, double-click the Graphics box that contains the image.

Once you get into WP Draw, use the tools in the toolbox (see Figure 2 below) or equivalent commands in the Draw and Attributes menus to create a new drawing or embellish an existing one. Look for instructions at the bottom of the screen after selecting a tool.

A summary of all the tools available on the pull-down menus appears below:

   File: Contains general commands for inserting, closing, and adjusting the drawing.

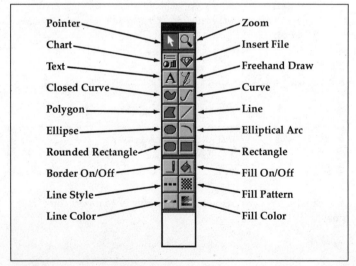

Figure 2:   The WordPerfect Draw Toolbox

Edit: Contains general commands for selecting, cutting, pasting, rotating, and so forth.

View: Lets you hide/display the ruler, grid, and button bar and lets you Zoom in and out on the drawing. Also lets you customize the grid snap.

Arrange: Includes options for contouring text and rearranging components of the drawing.

Draw: Provides the same drawing tools as the toolbox.

Text: Lets you insert and format text in the drawing and add the date and time.

Attributes: Lets you change the color, fill, line, and other attributes of the currently selected item, as well as for items you're about to draw.

Window: Contains standard Windows commands for arranging and choosing windows.

Help: Provides help specific to WordPerfect Draw.

To Save/Abandon a Drawing

When you're finished creating or modifying a drawing:

1. Choose File ➤ Exit And Return To Document.

2. If you want to save your changes, choose Yes. Otherwise, choose No.

 NOTES If you're not an artist and you use pre-drawn clip art often, you might prefer the much simpler Image Tools, discussed under Graphics Editor.

Though readily accessible from WordPerfect for Windows, WP Draw is actually a separate application. For more information on Draw, please refer to the WordPerfect Draw Booklet that came with your WordPerfect program.

SEE ALSO *Chart, Graphics and Graphics Boxes, TextArt*

ENVELOPE

Use the Envelope feature to type up an envelope easily.

To Type an Envelope

1. If available, select the text for the mailing address and then choose <u>L</u>ayout ➤ En<u>v</u>elope or click the Envelope button on the WordPerfect button bar.

2. Optionally, fill in the <u>R</u>eturn Address portion of the Envelope dialog box and select (check) Print Ret<u>u</u>rn Address. If you've created envelopes in the past in WordPerfect, you can choose to:

- Accept the current return address.

- Select an address from the drop-down list.

- Select <New Address> from the drop-down list and type in a new address.

- Add the current address to the drop-down list by choosing the <u>A</u>dd button.

- Delete an address from the drop-down list by highlighting that address in the drop-down list, choosing the D<u>e</u>lete button, and choosing <u>Y</u>es.

- Change the font for the address by choosing the <u>F</u>ont button and selecting a font (see the Font entry).

- Hide the return address by deselecting (unchecking) the Print Return Address option if it is already selected.

3. Fill in the <u>M</u>ailing Addresses box if you didn't select text for the mailing address in step 1. The procedure is basically the same as for filling in a return address, except that you choose options in the right side of the dialog box.

4.   If you wish, choose any of the options below:

- To *change the envelope size,* select a size from the Envelope Definitions drop-down list.

- To *create a new envelope size,* choose Create New Definition, specify the paper size options for an envelope including a Paper Name, and choose OK.

- *To print a POSTNET Bar Code* above the mailing address, choose Options, select (check) Include USPS POSTNET Bar Code, and choose OK. Until you deselect the option, WordPerfect will retrieve the POSTNET Bar Code from the mailing address automatically.

- To *change the position of the return or mailing addresses* on the envelope, choose Options, adjust the horizontal and vertical position of the appropriate address, and choose OK. WordPerfect will use the selected positions whenever you use the current envelope definition.

5.   If you want to print your envelope immediately, choose Print Envelope. If you want to save the envelope information in the current document (without printing), choose Append To Doc.

If you chose to print your envelope in step 5, insert the envelope into the printer according to your printer manual's instructions.

 SEE ALSO   *Bar Code, Paper Size*

EQUATIONS

The Equation Editor lets you create, edit, and align mathematical and scientific equations.

To Create an Equation

1. Move the cursor where you want the equation to appear in the document and choose Graphics ➤ Equation. You'll be taken to the Equation Editor.

2. Type the equation in the top half of the window, or use the Commands pop-up list to choose an Equation Palette, then double-click on the element you want to select in the Equation Palette.

3. To check your progress, choose View ➤ Redisplay (Ctrl+F3) or click the Redisplay button in the button bar.

4. When you've finished, choose File ➤ Close (Ctrl+F4) or click the Close button in the button bar.

To Edit an Equation

• Double-click the equation you want to change in the document window to get back to the Equation Editor.

To Delete an Equation

• Drag the Box code off of Reveal Codes or click the equation once, then press Delete (Del).

NOTES To control how elements of the equation are arranged, enclose portions of the equation in curly braces, as in the example below.

Equation Typed As...	Is Displayed As...
A+B OVER X+Y	$A + \dfrac{B}{X} + Y$
{A+B} OVER {X+Y}	$\dfrac{A+B}{X+Y}$

The Equation Editor lets you edit and select font options for equations with all the special symbols and typesetting standards. However, it does not solve the equations for you.

SEE ALSO *Characters, Graphics and Graphics Boxes*

EXIT

The Exit command closes WordPerfect and returns you to the Program Manager. You should always save your work and exit WordPerfect prior to turning off your computer.

To Exit WordPerfect

1. Choose File ➤ Exit or press Alt+F4.

2. If you have made changes to any open document, the prompt "Save changes to <filename>?" appears. Choose Yes to save, No to exit without saving the current file, or Cancel to abandon the operation and stay in WordPerfect.

3. If you chose Yes in step 2 and the file has yet to be saved, the Save As dialog box will appear. Enter a file name and choose OK.

To Exit the Current Document

• Choose File ➤ Close (Ctrl+F4).

If you have made changes to the document since the last time you saved it and do not want those changes to take effect, then answer No to the Save changes to Document? prompt.

 NOTES If you have multiple documents open when you exit WordPerfect, you will be prompted to save each document that has been modified since last saved.

SEE ALSO *Save/Save As*

Feature bars provide shortcuts for specific WordPerfect features and pop up only when they're needed. For example, when you choose Insert ➤ Comment ➤ Create, you'll see the Comment feature bar shown below.

The following feature bars appear when you choose the related menu options or shortcuts: Table Formula, Outline, Index, Table Of Contents, List, Cross-Reference, Table Of Authorities, Hypertext, Graphics Box, Header/Footer, Footnote/Endnote, Watermark, Merge, Template, Comment, Sound, ToA Full Form, Delay Codes, Caption, Text Box, Macro Edit.

To Use a Feature Bar

- Click the button you want, or hold down the Alt and Shift keys while you press the underlined letter in the button name. For example, you can select the Close button by clicking it, or by pressing Alt+Shift+C.

NOTES   You can't customize the appearance of feature bars, nor can you move them.

To find out what a button on the feature bar does, move the mouse pointer to the button and look at the WordPerfect title bar.

The following buttons appear in every feature bar:

? Click this button if you want to select a different feature bar or if you want to choose options from a menu instead of clicking buttons on the feature bar. Right-click this button (or the feature bar) to select a different feature bar or get help.

C̲lose   Choose this button when you're done using the feature bar and want to clear it from the screen. In some cases, choosing C̲lose also will close whatever editing window you're using.

 SEE ALSO   *Button Bar, Power Bar*

FILE MANAGEMENT

WordPerfect 6 for Windows does not have its own dedicated built-in file manager. However, you can manage files through the Open File and Save As dialog boxes. The dialog box in Figure 3 is typical of what you might see when opening or saving a file.

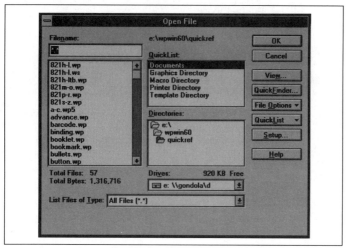

Figure 3: The Open File dialog box

To Manage Files

1. Choose File ➤ Open (Ctrl+O) or click the Open button on the Power Bar.

2. If necessary, choose a drive from the drop-down list, a directory, or Quick List.

3. Select the name of the file(s) you want to copy, move, delete, or whatever (see below).

4. Choose File Options, and then select whichever option is appropriate to what you want to do (i.e., Copy, Move, Rename, Delete, and so forth). See Options, below.

5. Follow any prompts or instructions on the screen. Choose OK to close the dialog box when you're done.

To Search for a Document

If the file you're looking for is on another *drive* and/or *directory*, you can search for it:

1. Go to a dialog box that opens or saves a file. For example, choose File ➤ Open.

2. To list a different group of file names in the File List Display, use any of the methods below:

- If the file is on a different drive, choose the drive you want from the Drives drop-down list.

- If the file is on a different directory, choose the directory you want from the Directories list. (For example, double-click the directory you want or highlight it and press ↵.)

- To list files of a different type, from the Open File dialog box select List Files of Type drop-down list and select a file type. Choose the top entry in the list if you want to display all files (*.*). Or specify a type in the Filename text box on the Save As dialog box.

- To specify the drive, directory, and file type all at once, type the full path name and wildcards into the text box above the list of files and press ⏎. For example, typing **c:\wpwin60\wpdocs\e*.*** into the box would list all files in the \WPWIN60\WPDOCS directory on drive C that start with **e**.

3. When the list shows the file name you want to work with, you can do any of the following:

    - Click on or use the arrow keys to highlight the file name in the file list. The highlighted file name will appear in the text box above the file list. Then click OK in the dialog box.

    - Double-click the file name you want. This completes the operation you chose in step 1 (for example, to open the file).

To Select More than One File

Use standard Windows techniques (summarized below) to select multiple files in the file list. After selecting the files, choose OK (to open up to nine files) or use the File Options button to manage the files. (See Options, below.)

- To select several adjacent file names, click the first file name (or highlight it and press the spacebar). Then hold down Shift and click the last file or press ↓ until you highlight the last file.

- To select several non-adjacent file names with the mouse, click on the first file name, then hold down Ctrl while clicking each additional file name.

- To deselect multiple selected files, click on any file name or press the spacebar.

- To deselect one file without deselecting others, hold down Ctrl and click on the file name you want to deselect. Or, press Shift+F8, use the ↑ or ↓ key to select the file name you want to deselect, and press the spacebar. When you are finished, press Shift+F8 again.

To Use the File Button

Many text boxes that allow you to enter a file or directory name have a file button at one end. If you're not sure of the file or directory name (or don't wish to type it), click the file button or move the cursor to the text box and press Alt+↓. A Select File or Select Directory dialog box will open. Use the techniques described above to locate the name you want, then double-click the name or highlight it and choose OK to return to the original dialog box.

OPTIONS Most or all of these buttons are available in dialog boxes that open or save files:

View Opens the Viewer window, which lets you look at most files without opening them first. To see what's in a file, select it and click the View button, and it will appear in the Viewer window. Maximize, restore, resize, or close the Viewer window as needed. To search through the file shown, click on the Viewer window and press F2 to open the Find dialog box. (See the Find entry for more information.) Right-click the Viewer Window to display a QuickMenu of Search options.

QuickFinder Lets you use QuickFinder to locate files that contain certain text. (See the QuickFinder entry for more information.)

Quicklist Lets you choose whether the directory list includes the directory list, QuickList, or both; and lets you edit the QuickList. (See the QuickList entry for more information.)

File Options Lets you choose from these file management commands: Copy (copies one or more files), Move (moves one or more files to a new location), Rename (renames one or more files), Delete (deletes one or more files), Change Attributes (changes file attributes of one or more files, Print (prints one or more WordPerfect files), Print List (prints a list of selected file names or the entire list of file names), Create Directory (creates a new directory), Remove Directory (deletes the highlighted directory in the Directories list, or whichever directory you specify). Instead of choosing File Options ➤ Delete, you can press the Del key.

Help Provides help on file management operations.

NOTES   You can also use the Windows File Manager to manage files. Press Alt+Tab until you get to the Program Manager, then open the Main group and open File Manager. See your Windows documentation for more information.

SEE ALSO   *Combine Documents, Find, New, Open, Quick-Finder, QuickList, Save/Save As*

FIND

This command lets you locate a particular character, phrase, or code in your document.

To Use Find

1.   Move the cursor to where you want to begin the search, then choose Edit ➤ Find or press F2.

   • If you want to search for a particular word or phrase, type the text you're looking for.

   • To include a special character in the search, press Ctrl+W and add the character as you normally would when typing a document.

   • To search for a general code, choose Match ➤ Codes and select the code(s) you want to look for. Then choose Insert in the Codes dialog box.

   • To search for a specific code, choose Type ➤ Specific Codes, select the code you want to search for, then click OK in the Specific Codes dialog box.

   • To make the search more specific, choose Match, then choose Whole Word, Case, and/or Font as appropriate.

2. When you've defined the text and/or codes you're searching for, choose Find Next to search forward or Find Prev to search backward from the position of the cursor.

3. When you're done searching, choose Close to close the Find Text dialog box.

To repeat the previous search after you've closed the Find Text dialog box, press Shift+F2 to search forward or Alt+F2 to search backward.

 SEE ALSO   *Font, Go To, Replace*

FONT

Use the Font command to change the typeface, size, and appearance of any text in your document.

To Select a Font or Attribute

1. Move the cursor where you want to make the change. Or, if you want to change the font/attribute of existing text, select that text.

2. Choose Layout ➤ Font (F9), then choose a Font Face, Font Style, Font Size, Appearance, Position, Relative Size, and optionally Color from the Font dialog box.

3. Choose OK to return to your document.

If you selected text in step 1, only that text will be displayed with the new attribute or font in the new font. If you didn't select text, all text beyond the cursor will appear in the new font until the font code is inserted in the document.

NOTES   WordPerfect cannot create fonts. It can only use fonts that are built into your printer and fonts that you've purchased and installed separately. Typically, you use Windows (rather than WordPerfect) to install optional third-party fonts.

 SEE ALSO   *Font Setup, Selecting Text*

FONT SETUP

Use Font Setup to take advantage of today's modern graphics fonts such as TrueType (which is built into windows) or Type 1 (through the Adobe Type Manager, abbreviated as ATMl). You can also use Font Setup to install older printer fonts from cartridges and down-loadable soft fonts.

To Install Graphics Fonts

To install graphics fonts, follow the font manufacturer's instructions. The fonts will be installed in your Windows printer drivers.

If you're installing TrueType fonts and need help, refer to your Windows documentation. You may need to use the Font applet in the Windows Control Panel to install and activate the fonts.

To Install Printer Fonts

To install non-graphics fonts such as cartridges and downloadable soft fonts, follow the font manufacturer's instructions.

If you can't get to your printer fonts from WordPerfect, it's probably because WordPerfect doesn't know they're available. Follow these steps so WordPerfect can use your fonts:

1.   Choose File ➤ Select Printer and click on the name of the printer to which you want to install fonts.

2.   Choose Setup. You'll be taken to that printer's setup dialog box.

- If you're installing soft fonts to a WordPerfect printer driver, make sure the Path For Downloadable Fonts And Printer Commands option specifies the drive and directory of the soft fonts. Then choose Cartridges/Fonts and select fonts as instructed on the screen.

- If you're installing fonts for a Windows printer driver, follow instructions in the Printer manual.

3.   When you're done, choose OK and Close as necessary to work your way back to the Document window.

 SEE ALSO   *Font*

FOOTNOTES AND ENDNOTES

Use footnotes or endnotes to list sources or provide more detailed information on an item in your text. Footnotes print at the bottom of the page where they are referenced. Endnotes are usually placed at the end of the document. Because footnote and endnote commands work almost identically, we'll refer to them as *notes*.

To Create a Note

1.   Position the cursor to the right of the text to be marked with a note number.

2.   Choose Insert ➤ Footnote or Insert ➤ Endnote, then choose Create.

3. Type the text of your note.

4. Choose Close from the feature bar when you are finished.

To Edit a Note

1. Choose Insert ➤ Footnote or Insert ➤ Endnote. Or double-click the hidden [Footnote] or [Endnote] code on Reveal Codes.

2. Enter the number, character, or letter of the note you want to edit. Then click OK or press ⏎.

3. Edit the note.

4. Choose Close when you are finished.

To Delete a Note

1. Turn on Reveal Codes (Alt+F3) and locate the hidden code for the note you want to delete.

2. Drag that code out of Reveal Codes into the document window.

To Customize Notes

1. Move the cursor so it's before the first note that you want to customize.

2. Choose Insert ➤ Footnote or Insert ➤ Endnote, then choose New Number if you want to renumber the notes or Options if you want to change the appearance or over-all numbering scheme. If you're customizing Endnotes, you can also choose Placement to determine where the end notes will appear in your document.

NOTES WordPerfect automatically numbers and formats notes and places them in your document. Notes in Master Documents are numbered as if you were using one large document.

Notes are not visible on the screen when you're using Draft view.

SEE ALSO *Reveal Codes*

FORCE PAGE

Use this feature to force a page to start on an odd or even page number.

To Force an Odd/Even Page

1. Move the cursor to the top of the page that you want to ensure is odd- or even-numbered.

2. Choose Layout ➤ Page ➤ Force Page, then whichever option is appropriate to your needs. Choose OK to return to the document window.

 SEE ALSO *Page Breaks*

GENERATE

Generate compiles tables of contents, tables of authorities, indexes, lists, and cross-references automatically. Before using generate, you must mark appropriate entries in your document.

To Generate Reference
Tables, Indexes, and Lists

1. Choose Tools ➤ Generate (Ctrl+F9). If you wish, choose Options, then Select Save Subdocuments and/or Build Hypertext Links and choose OK.

2. Choose OK.

NOTES   Once you've started Generate, the status bar keeps you informed of its progress.

SEE ALSO   *Cross-Reference, Index, Lists, Master Document, Table of Authorities, Table of Contents*

GO TO

Go To lets you move the cursor to a specific position in a document, a specific newspaper or parallel column, or a position within selected text.

To Use Go To

1. Choose <u>E</u>dit ➤ <u>G</u>o To (Ctrl+G).

2. Choose the position you want to move to or enter a page number, bookmark, or Table Cell/Range, then choose OK.

 SEE ALSO *Columns, Find, Selecting Text*

GRAMMATIK

Grammatik (rhymes with *dramatic*) is a utility that checks the grammar, spelling, and writing style of WordPerfect documents.

To Start Grammatik

1. Move the cursor to where you want to start checking grammar, or select the text you want to check.

2. Choose <u>T</u>ools ➤ <u>G</u>rammatik, or click on Grammatik in the power bar. Optionally, select Chec<u>k</u> and indicate the amount of text (for instance, a sentence, paragraph, or entire document) that you want to check.

3. You can also select <u>O</u>ptions and choose a writing style, checking options (such as disabling the spell checker), and so forth, then choose OK. (See Options, below.)

4. Choose <u>S</u>tart when you're ready to start checking. When Grammatik finds an error (or what it thinks is an error), it displays a message indicating the type of error it discovered. You can then:

- Drag the Grammatik window by its title bar to some other area of the screen (if you can't see the error in your document).

- Click in the document window and make your changes immediately. Then click the Resume button.

- Choose Skip if you don't want to make changes to the selected text.

- Choose Next Sentence if you want to move to the next sentence.

If you didn't disable Grammatik's spell checker in step 3 above and Grammatik finds a misspelling, you can also:

- Choose Replace (if available) to change the selected word to the suggested word.

- Choose Ignore Word if you don't want Grammatik to count that word as a misspelling for the rest of the current check.

- Choose Add if you want to add the current word to Grammatik's speller dictionary so it won't ever be counted as a misspelling in the future.

When you've finished with Grammatik, choose Close to close its window.

OPTIONS   Select any of the following items in the options dialog box. Use the Options ➤ Checking Options command to display the dialog box.

Check for paragraph errors: Turn on to check for one-sentence paragraphs and headings. Must be turned on for WordPerfect to compute paragraph statistics.

Ignore periods within words: Grammatik will skip DOS filenames and other words containing periods.

Suggest spelling replacements: When on, provides suggestions for detected spelling errors. When off, double-click (Suggest) or click the Suggest button for a list of suggested words.

Start checking immediately: Checking starts as soon as Grammatik is opened, with all the default settings accepted.

 SEE ALSO *Speller, Thesaurus*

GRAPHICS AND GRAPHICS BOXES

The Graphics and Graphics boxes features let you add pictures or equations to your document.

To Create a Graphics Box

1. Move the cursor to where you want to put the graphics image.

2. Choose Graphics ➤ Figure.

3. If necessary, use the QuickList and/or Drives and Directories lists to switch to the directory on which the graphics image is stored.

4. Click the name of the graphics image to insert, then choose OK.

The image will appear in a Figure box, typically about 3.25" wide, anchored to the current paragraph, and aligned with the right margin.

To Size or Position a Graphics Box

- Use your mouse to drag the box to its new location

- Click the box once and drag one of its sizing handles until the box is the desired size.

- For more precise positioning, right-click the box, choose
  <u>P</u>osition, <u>S</u>ize, or <u>W</u>rap, as appropriate, and define the
  box's position, size, and text wrap options.

To Fill a Graphics Box

To change the contents of a graphics box:

1. Right-click the box and choose C<u>o</u>ntent, then:

- To put a graphic image from the disk into the box, click
  the button next to the <u>F</u>ilename text box and choose the
  drive, directory, and file name of the graphic image to
  insert. Then select OK.

- To put text or a table into the box, choose <u>T</u>ext from the
  <u>C</u>ontent pop-up list, choose <u>Y</u>es to replace the current
  contents, then choose <u>E</u>dit. Create your table and/or
  type your text. Choose fonts, justification, and other formatting features in the usual manner. Choose <u>C</u>lose
  from the feature bar when you're done.

- If you want the box to be empty, choose <u>E</u>mpty from
  the pop-up list next to <u>C</u>ontent; if necessary, select <u>Y</u>es
  to delete the current contents, then choose OK.

To Change the Box Style or Appearance

There are three ways to change the border and the general appearance of a graphics box:

- To change the borders on the current box only, right-click
  the box, choose <u>B</u>order/Fill, design your border, and
  choose OK.

- To switch the box to a different box style, right-click the
  box, choose S<u>t</u>yle, then choose the type of box to which
  you want to convert the current box.

- To change the appearance of all the boxes in a given
  category (e.g., all the Figure boxes or all the User
  boxes), choose <u>G</u>raphics ➤ Graphics Styles. Select <u>O</u>p-
  tions, then <u>S</u>etup ➤ <u>C</u>urrent Document ➤ OK. In the

Styles list box, choose the type of box you want to re-design, then choose Edit. Design the box style from the options given, then choose OK and Close to work your way back to the document window.

To Create or Edit a Caption

1. Right-click the box for which you want to create or edit a caption, then:

- To create or edit the text of a caption, select Create Caption or Edit Caption as appropriate, type or edit your caption, then choose Close from the feature bar.

- To change the position, rotation, or style of the caption, choose Caption and use the options that appear in the Box Caption dialog box. Then choose OK.

To Renumber Boxes

Graphics boxes are numbered consecutively throughout the document by box type. When you create a caption for most box types, the automatic number appears at the start of the caption. To change the numbering of boxes:

1. Display the Reveal Codes Screen (Alt+F3) and move the cursor to just before the hidden code for the first box you want
renumbered.

2. Choose Insert ➤ Other ➤ Counter and highlight the type of box you want to renumber.

3. Choose Value and enter the new starting number for the boxes, or use any of the other available options to increase or decrease the number, and choose OK.

Alternatively, you can choose Edit from the Counter Numbering dialog box to switch to some other numbering method such as letters (A, B, C, D) or roman numerals I, II, III, IV).

4.   Click OK and Close as necessary to return to the document window.

OPTIONS   When you're positioning a graphics box, you can choose from the following anchor options:

Put Box On Current Page (Page Anchor)   Lets you define a specific place on the page to put the box. Text will flow around the box.

Put Box In Current Paragraph (Paragraph Anchor)   The box will be attached to its nearest paragraph and will float with that paragraph. That is, if you insert or delete text above the paragraph that the box is anchored to, the box will move automatically to stay attached to its neighboring paragraph.

Treat Box As Character (Character Anchor)   The box is anchored to its nearest character and moves along with that character as you insert and delete other text.

Place   Positions the box horizontally from a specified location.

Place   Positions the box vertically from a specified location.

 NOTES   There are eight different types of graphic boxes: Figure, Text, Equation, Table, User, Button, Watermark, and Inline Equation. However, all graphic boxes are virtually the same. The type of box you choose only defines the initial appearance of the box and the numbering system to use. For example, your document might contain Figure boxes numbered 1, 2, etc., but it might also contain Table boxes numbered 1, 2, etc.

SEE ALSO   *Graphics Editor, Styles*

GRAPHICS EDITOR

The graphics image editor lets you make changes to existing clip art.

To Use the Graphics Editor

1. Right-click the graphics box you want to change and choose Image Tools. The toolbox shown below in Figure 4 appears:

Figure 4: Graphics Editor Toolbox

2. Make your changes using the available tools, then click in the document window outside the graphics box.

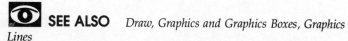 **NOTES**   If the Image Tools palette overlays the graphic image, drag the horizontal bar at the top of the palette to a clear area. To close the Image Tools palette, double-click its upper-left corner.

SEE ALSO   *Draw, Graphics and Graphics Boxes, Graphics Lines*

GRAPHICS LINES

The Graphics Lines command allows you to put graphics lines anywhere in your document. Be aware that you can only print graphics
lines with a graphics printer.

To Create a Graphics Line

1. Move the cursor to where you want the line to appear.

2. Choose Graphics, then choose either Horizontal Line
(Ctrl+F11) for a horizontal line that runs from the left to
the right margin, Vertical Line (Ctrl+Shift+F11) for a vertical line that runs from the top to bottom margin, or Custom Line for any other type of line.

3. If you chose Custom Line in step 2, you can now define
the style, type, position, length, etc., by choosing options
from the Create Graphics Line dialog box that appears.
Choose OK when you're done.

To Change a Graphics Line

• Click the line so that it has sizing handles, then drag the
entire line to a new location or drag just the sizing handles
to change the length or thickness of the line.

• Or, double-click the line, or right-click the line and choose
Edit Horizontal (or Vertical) Line to get to the Edit Graphics Line dialog box.

To Delete a Line

Click the line once, then press Delete (Del).

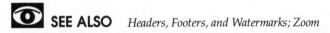**NOTES** If you select Do Not Print Graphics from the Print dialog box just before printing, the lines won't be printed.

If you have trouble selecting the graphics line with the mouse, zoom in to 200% and then click it.

SEE ALSO *Headers, Footers, and Watermarks; Zoom*

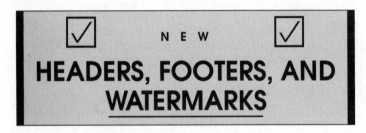

You can print *repeating elements* at the top (headers), bottom (footers), or behind the text (watermarks) of every page, odd pages only, or even pages only. Watermarks are pale gray and are covered by the text and graphics on a page.

To Create or Edit a Repeating Element

1. Move the cursor to the top of the page where the repeating element should take effect.

2. To create or edit a header or footer, choose Layout ➤ Header/Footer. To create or edit a watermark, choose Layout ➤ Watermark.

3. Choose Header A, Header B, Footer A, Footer B, Watermark A, or Watermark B.

4. Choose Create or Edit.

5. Type or edit the header or footer and choose any options you want (see Notes and Options, below).

6. Choose Close on the feature bar to return to the document window.

To Discontinue a Repeating Element

1. Position the cursor on the page where you want to discontinue the repeating element.

2. Choose Layout ➤ Header/Footer or Layout ➤ Watermark.

3. Choose Header A, Header B, Footer A, Footer B, Watermark A, or Watermark B.

4. Choose Discontinue.

OPTIONS   These options are available on the Header/Footer or Watermark feature bar:

Close Closes the editing window and hides the feature bar.

Distance Controls the distance between the text and repeating element. (Headers and footers only.)

Figure Inserts a graphics image at the cursor position. (Watermarks only.)

File Inserts a file at the cursor position. (Watermarks only.)

Line Inserts a horizontal or vertical line at the cursor position. (Headers and footers only.)

Next Edits the next repeating element of the same type (e.g., the next Header A).

Number Inserts a page, secondary page, chapter, or volume number at the cursor position. (Headers and footers only.)

Placement Places the repeating element on Odd Pages, Even Pages, or Every Page (default).

Previous Edits the previous repeating element of the same type (e.g., the previous Header A).

NOTES You can define up to two headers (A and B), two footers (A and B), and two watermarks (A and B) per document page to use at any time, and you can change them as needed. A repeating element will remain in effect until you define a different repeating element, suppress it (see the Suppress entry), discontinue it, or delete it.

WordPerfect automatically adds an extra line after a header and before a footer.

Repeating elements may contain up to one page of text.

Repeating elements appear in Page or Two-Page view, but not in Draft view.

To delete a repeating element, turn on Reveal Codes (Alt+F3) and drag the appropriate [Header], [Footer], or [Watermark] code into the document window.

To edit a repeating element quickly, turn on Reveal Codes (Alt+F3) and double-click the appropriate [Header], [Footer], or [Watermark] code.

While editing a repeating element, you can use all the usual features of WordPerfect, including graphics, fonts, Speller, Thesaurus, Insert ➤ Date, and Insert ➤ Other, as well as buttons in the feature bar (see Options, above).

SEE ALSO *Delay Codes, Page Numbering, Suppress*

HELP

Like all Windows applications, WordPerfect provides both general and context-sensitive help. General help explains basic WordPerfect tasks. Context-sensitive help pertains to the task you're doing or to a specific region of the screen.

To Access Help

Choose options from the Help menu, press F1, click the Help button (if it's available in a dialog box), or press Shift+F1 and click on an area of the screen. The results of pressing F1 depend on what was active when you pressed it:

- From a document window, the Help contents appear.

- From the Help window, information about how to use Help appears.

- From active menu items, dialog boxes, or special windows (such as Speller), specific information about the item appears.

To Find Help Topics

Use any method below to find information on a topic:

- Choose Help ➤ Contents from the menu bar, then click the Help section you want.

- Choose Help ➤ Search For Help On from the menu bar, or click the Search button while in a Help window. Type a word or scroll to locate the topic, then double-click the topic. In the lower window, scroll to the topic you want, then double-click it.

- Choose Help ➤ How Do I from the menu bar and select a common task from the available categories.

- Choose a *jump* word, indicated by colored or underlined text or as a graphic, from the help text to look up topics related to the current one.

To Exit Help

- Choose File ➤ Exit, or double-click the Help window's Control-menu box, or click the Help window's Close button.

To Print Help Information

Open the Help window you want to print, then…

1.   Choose File ➤ Print Setup (if necessary), set the options you need, and choose OK.

2.   Choose File ➤ Print Topic.

 NOTES   To find out more about macros, choose Help ➤ Macros from the menu bar.

Two of WordPerfect's Help menu options will get you up and running fast. These are Help ➤ Coach and Help ➤ Tutorial, both available from the WordPerfect menu bar.

Help ➤ Coach takes you through an actual WordPerfect operation step by step. To use Coach, position the cursor where you want the operation to begin, choose Help ➤ Coach, select the option you want, and follow the prompts on the screen.

Help ➤ Tutorial runs an interactive tutorial that shows you how to use basic WordPerfect features.

Help ➤ About WordPerfect displays the current version of Word-Perfect, the license number, and other information.

SEE ALSO   *Your WordPerfect 6.0 for Windows manual*

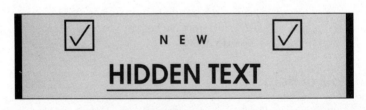

N E W

HIDDEN TEXT

The Hidden Text feature prevents selected text from being displayed on the screen or printed.

To Hide Text

1. Select the text, fonts, attributes, lines, graphics, or other information that you want to hide.

2. Choose <u>L</u>ayout ➤ <u>F</u>ont (or press F9).

3. Select (check) Hidd<u>e</u>n under Appearance in the Font dialog box.

4. Choose OK.

To Display Hidden Text

Choose <u>V</u>iew ➤ Hidden Te<u>x</u>t to display hidden text. You can now edit and print it as you would any normal text. To hide the text once more, choose <u>V</u>iew ➤ Hidden Te<u>x</u>t again.

To Delete Hidden Text

Choose <u>V</u>iew ➤ Reveal <u>C</u>odes (Alt+F3), then delete the [Hidden] code at the beginning or end of the hidden text.

 NOTES   Hidden text is useful for writing notes to yourself or hiding information that you might want to display and print later.

When hidden text is visible, WordPerfect treats it like any other information in your document.

You can hide any text, graphics, fonts, or codes between the [Hidden] codes.

SEE ALSO   *Comment, Font*

This command allows you to hide WordPerfect's button bar, power bar, ruler bar, status bar, and menu bar in a single step.

To Hide All the Bars

Choose View ➤ Hide Bars or press Alt+Shift+F5, then choose OK.

To Redisplay the Bars

Press Esc or Alt+V, then select Hide Bars or press Alt+Shift+F5 again.

 NOTES   To display or hide individual bars, choose any of the following options from the View menu: Button Bar, Power Bar, Ruler Bar (Alt+Shift+F3), or Status Bar. All these options are toggles: when selected (checked), the bar is visible; when deselected, the bar is hidden.

You can also hide a bar by right-clicking the bar and choosing "Hide...Bar" from the QuickMenu.

SEE ALSO   *Button Bar, Power Bar, Ruler, Status Bar*

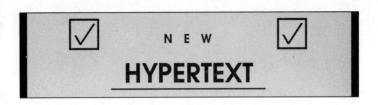

Hypertext is a *hot spot* that you put into your documents. The hot spot, which is either a section of colored, underlined text (like the *jump words* in Help) or a command button, will perform some action when clicked. For example, clicking on a hot spot could open a document, jump to a bookmark, or do anything else a macro can do.

Hypertext features are available when the Hypertext feature bar is visible.

To Display or Hide the Hypertext Feature Bar

- To display the feature bar, choose Tools ➤ Hypertext.

- To hide the feature bar, choose the Close button in the feature bar.

To Create or Change a Hypertext Hot Spot

1. Create the WordPerfect document, bookmark, or macro you want the hot spot to jump *to.*

2. If you're creating hypertext, select the text you want to jump *from.* If you're changing hypertext, move the cursor just past the underlined text or button. (In Reveal Codes, the cursor should be just past the [Hypertext End] code.)

3. Display the Hypertext feature bar.

4. Click the Create or Edit button in the feature bar.

5. Select an action and fill in the text box. Your options are Go To Bookmark, Go To Other Document and Bookmark, and Run Macro.

6. Select an appearance, either Text or Button.

7. Choose OK.

To Jump to and from Hypertext

1. Display the Hypertext feature bar and move the cursor to the hypertext link you want to jump from.

2. If the Active button in visible, click it. The button changes to Deactivate.

3. Click the link you are jumping from. The cursor moves to the bookmark or document, or the macro runs.

4. Choose the Back button on the feature bar to return to the original hypertext button.

5. Choose the Next button to jump to the next link. Choose the Previous button to move to the previous link.

To Edit the Hypertext Text or Button

1. Display the Hypertext feature bar.

2. Make sure the Activate/Deactivate button says Activate.

3. Edit the text as if it were normal text, or edit the button as you would any graphic box.

4. When you're done making changes, click the Activate button in the feature bar (its name changes back to Deactivate).

To Delete Hypertext

1. Position the cursor just before the hypertext to be deleted.

2. Display the Hypertext feature bar.

3. Click the Delete button in the feature bar. (Choose Edit ➤ Undo or press Ctrl+Z immediately if you want to recover deleted hypertext.)

To Generate Hypertext Links

Build hypertext links when you generate lists for a master document.

1. Choose Tools ➤ Generate or press Ctrl+F9, then choose Options.

2. Select (check) Build Hypertext Links to build the links; deselect the option to generate the lists without building links first (this will be faster). Choose OK twice to start generating the lists.

NOTES   To deactivate hypertext, click the Deactivate button in the feature bar. You must deactivate hypertext before you can change the underlined text or appearance of the button at the hot spot.

To activate hypertext, click the Activate button in the feature bar.

If hypertext is active, you can jump to a hot spot by clicking on it, even if the Hypertext feature bar isn't visible. To jump back, however, you'll need to display the Hypertext feature bar and click the Back button.

SEE ALSO   *Bookmark, Feature Bar, Generate, Graphics and Graphics Boxes, List, Macros, Sound*

HYPHENATION

Hyphenation adds a smoother, more professional look to your document by automatically hyphenating words at the end of lines that would contain too much white space if the whole word was wrapped. You can hyphenate words manually or let WordPerfect do it for you. It's easiest to turn hyphenation on or off and use default settings for other hyphenation options (see Notes, below).

To Turn Automatic Hyphenation On and Off

1. Position the cursor where you want to turn hyphenation on or off.

2. Choose Layout ➤ Line ➤ Hyphenation.

3. Select (check) Hyphenation On to turn hyphenation on. Deselect Hyphenation On to turn hyphenation off.

4. Choose OK.

To Respond to Hyphenation Prompts

If WordPerfect needs your help during automatic hyphenation, the word that needs hyphenation will appear in the Position Hyphen dialog box. Position the hyphen in the word by clicking the mouse where you want the hyphen to appear, or by using the ← and → keys. Then click Insert Hyphen.

If you prefer not to insert a hyphen when prompted for hyphenation help, you can choose other options in the Position Hyphen dialog box:

- To prevent the word from being hyphenated now or later and to wrap the word to the next line, choose Ignore Word.

- To stop hyphenating words temporarily, choose Suspend Hyphenation.

- To insert a hyphenation soft return instead of a hyphen at the hyphenation point, choose Hyphenation SRt.

- To insert a space instead of a hyphen at the hyphenation point, choose Insert Space.

To Hyphenate Manually

1. Position the cursor where you want the character or code to appear.

2. Type the character or code (if it's available on the keyboard), or choose Layout ➤ Line ➤ Other codes.

3. Select a hyphenation option from the Other Codes dialog box and choose Insert.

Table II lists various hyphenation characters, codes, and information on how to type them into a word.

Table II: A Summary of Hyphens and Dashes

HYPHEN CHARACTER AND CODE	DESCRIPTION	KEYSTROKE*
Hyphen [- Hyphen]	Permanent (-) hyphen used to break two words at the end of a line. Use for words that normally include hyphens, such as *father-in-law*.	-
Soft hyphen [- Soft Hyphen]	Temporary hyphen that breaks a word only when necessary (WordPerfect uses this during automatic hyphenation).	Ctrl+Shift+-
Hard hyphen-	A dash (-) that's never separated at the end of a line. Use to insert a hyphen in words that shouldn't break at the end of a line, such as *tip-top*.	Ctrl+-
En dash [–:4,33]	A dash (–) that's never separated at the end of a line.	Ctrl+W n-
Em dash [—:4,34]	A dash (—) that's never separated at the end of a line.	Ctrl+W m-
Hyphenation soft return [Hyph SRt]	Breaks words at a certain place when hyphenation is needed, but doesn't display a hyphen.	Choose Layout ➤ Line ➤ Other Codes ➤ Hyphenation

Table II: A Summary of Hyphens and Dashes (continued)

HYPHEN CHARACTER AND CODE	DESCRIPTION	KEYSTROKE*
Soft Return ➤ ↵		
Ignore Word [Cancel Hyph]	Wraps the entire word to the next line and prevents future hyphenation.	Ctrl+/

*NOTE: *If you can't remember which character produces the hyphenation code, choose* Layout ➤ Line ➤ *Other Codes, select the character you want from the dialog box, and choose* ↵

To Set the Hyphenation Zone

WordPerfect uses the hyphenation zone to decide when to break a word during automatic hyphenation. There are two zones, one on each side of the right margin. Hyphenation zones are measured as a percentage of the line length. With hyphenation on, WordPerfect hyphenates words that start before the left zone and extend past the right zone.

1. Position the cursor where you want to change the hyphenation zone.

2. Choose Layout ➤ Line ➤ Hyphenation.

3. Enter the percentage of line length to use for the Left and Right hyphenation zones. Set a wide zone to hyphenate fewer words or a narrow zone to hyphenate more words.

4. Choose OK.

To Choose Hyphenation Environment Settings

Customize hyphenation by changing Environment Preferences settings.

1.   Choose File ➤ Preferences and double-click Environment.

2.   Choose any of the options below.

- To control how often you're prompted during automatic hyphenation, choose Hyphenation Prompt and select one of these options: Always (prompts when a word needs hyphenation); Never (never prompts for help; the entire word is wrapped to the next line if its hyphenation isn't found); When Required (prompts only if a word's hyphenation isn't found).

- To turn the beep on when WordPerfect needs hyphenation help, select (check) Hyphenation in the Beep On area. To turn off the beep, deselect Hyphenation.

3.   Choose OK, then Close.

NOTES   When hyphenation is off, WordPerfect wraps (moves) a word to the next line when the word extends beyond the right margin. When hyphenation is on, WordPerfect will hyphenate words as you type or scroll through existing text.

SEE ALSO   *Justification, Preferences*

INDENT

WordPerfect provides several ways to indent paragraphs or blocks of text.

To Indent a Paragraph

1.   Place the cursor where the indent should start. You can indent at existing text or where you're about to type.

2.   Press an indent key or choose one of the indent options
     listed below:

   - To indent the *first line* of a paragraph, press Tab.

   - To indent the *left margin*, press F7, choose Layout ➤
     Paragraph ➤ Indent, or click the Indent button on the
     WordPerfect button bar.

   - To indent the *left and right margins* by an equal amount,
     press Ctrl+Shift+F7, choose Layout ➤ Paragraph ➤
     Double Indent.

   - To insert a *hanging indent*, press Ctrl+F7 or choose Lay-
     out ➤ Paragraph ➤ Hanging Indent. A hanging indent
     keeps the first line in a paragraph flush with the left
     margin while indenting the remaining lines.

   - To insert a *margin release*, choose Layout ➤ Paragraph ➤
     Back Tab or press Shift+Tab. A margin release moves
     the cursor to the left by one tab stop. If the cursor is at
     the start of an indented line, that line returns to the left
     margin (like a hanging indent).

3.   If necessary, type the paragraph and press ↵.

To Create Numbered or Bulleted Indented Lists

You can create numbered or bulleted lists in which the text following the item number or bullet is indented (like lists in this book).

1.   Move the cursor to where the list should begin.

2.   Create your list as follows:

   - To create a list "manually," type the item number (e.g.,
     1.) or a bullet character (e.g., press Ctrl+W, type **, and
     press ↵). Press F7 or Ctrl+F7 to indent or double-
     indent. Type the text for the list item, then press ↵ once
     or twice. Repeat these steps as needed.

   - To create an automatic numbered or bulleted list, see
     the Bullets and Numbers entry.

- To create an outline, see the Outline entry.

NOTES Indentation is based on the current tab settings. Each time you indent, the indentation will move to the next tab stop.

When typing new text, indentation remains in effect until you press ↵ or insert a page break or column break (Ctrl+↵).

The Layout ➤ Paragraph ➤ Format commands provide another way to indent the left and right margin in paragraphs. (See the Paragraph entry.)

WordPerfect can automatically generate various lists such as lists of captioned figures. (See the List entry.)

SEE ALSO *Bullets and Numbers, List, Margins, Outline, Paragraph, Tabs*

INDEX

You can create an index for your document using WordPerfect's Index feature. This involves three basic steps. First, create a concordance file or mark index entries in your document. Second, define the index location and appearance. Third, generate the index.

Index features are available when the Index feature bar is visible.

To Display or Close the Index Feature Bar

- To display the feature bar, choose Tools ➤ Index.

- To hide the feature bar, choose the Close button in the feature bar.

To Create a Concordance File

A concordance file contains all the words and phrases that you want included in the index. When you define the index, you can have WordPerfect use the concordance file only or use the concordance file along with marked text within the document.

1. Open a blank document window (File ➤ New or Ctrl+N) or click the New Document button on the power bar.

2. Type a word or phrase to include in the index and press ↵. Repeat this step for each word or phrase you want to index.

3. Sort the list alphabetically to speed up index generation. Choose Tools ➤ Sort (Alt+F9), specify the sort keys, and choose OK.

4. Save the concordance file. Choose File ➤ Save (Ctrl+S) or click the Save button on the power bar, type a file name, and choose OK.

WordPerfect will generate an index entry whenever a phrase in the document *exactly* matches a phrase in the concordance file. Uppercase and lowercase entries (e.g., "TREES" and "trees") are treated the same.

To Mark Index Entries within a Document

1. Display the Index feature bar.

2. Select the word or phrase you want to index. (You can choose Edit ➤ Find or press F2 to locate words and phrases quickly.)

3. To specify the heading for this entry, click the Heading drop-down list button in the feature bar. The selected text will appear in the list. You can edit this if you wish, or select an existing heading from the list.

4. To specify the subheading for this entry (optional), click the Subheading drop-down list button. The selected text will appear in the list. You can edit this if you wish, or select an existing subheading from the list.

5. Click the Mark button in the feature bar.

6. Repeat steps 3–5 until you've entered and marked all the headings and subheadings for the selected text.

To mark additional entries in your document, repeat steps 2–6 for each word or phrase.

To Define the Index Location and Page Numbering Style

1. Move the cursor to where you want the index to appear (usually at the end of your document).

2. Optionally, press Ctrl+↵ to insert a page break.

3. Optionally, type a title for the index and press ↵.

4. Display the Index feature bar.

5. Click the Define button in the feature bar. The Define Index dialog box appears.

6. Choose any appearance options you want (see Options, below).

7. If you're using a concordance file, enter its name into the Filename text box, or use the filename button to locate the file.

8. Choose OK.

To Generate an Index

1. Display the Index feature bar.

2. Click the Generate button in the feature bar.

3. Choose OK.

OPTIONS   The following options in the Define Index dialog box control the appearance of index entries.

Position   Lets you define where the page number appears with respect to the text of the index entry.

Page Numbering   Lets you define the format of the page number.

Use Dash To Show Consecutive Pages   When selected (checked), a dash indicates consecutive page numbers. When deselected, each page number in a range is listed separately.

Change   Lets you change the style of the heading and sub-heading entries.

NOTES   You can mark the word or phrase being indexed as a heading or as both a heading and subheading.

The word or phrase being indexed need not match its heading or subheading. For example, in a book about wildlife observation, you might select the phrase "Identifying Tracks." Then, after choosing Heading on the feature bar, you could change the phrase to "Tracks, Identifying."

To delete an index entry in the document, choose View ➤ Reveal Codes (Alt+F3) and delete the appropriate [Index] code.

See the QuickFinder entry to learn about another type of index that can instantly show you which files contain a particular word or phrase.

Concordance file entries are automatically used as index headings. For more control over the headings and subheadings, you can mark concordance file entries as explained in "To Mark Index Entries within a Document" above.

SEE ALSO   *Find, Generate, List, Master Document, Page Numbering, QuickFinder, Sorting and Selecting, Styles, Table of Authorities, Table of Contents*

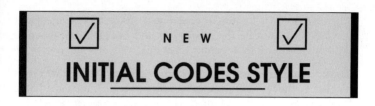

INITIAL CODES STYLE

N E W

The initial codes style is WordPerfect's default setting for a document's content and appearance. Any changes to it affect the current document only.

To Change the Initial Codes Style for a Document

1. Choose Layout ➤ Document ➤ Initial Codes Style. The Styles Editor dialog box appears.

2. In the Contents box, enter all the text, formatting codes, graphics, and other features you want to predefine. You can type text, use the Styles Editor pull-down menus, or press shortcut keys as needed. See the Styles entry for details.

3. Select the Use As Default checkbox to change the initial codes style for all subsequent documents.

4. Choose OK when you're done.

NOTES   You can define initial codes for nearly every WordPerfect feature (unavailable options will be grayed out in the menus).

The [Open Style:InitialStyle] code for the initial codes style always appears in the Reveal Codes screen at the start of each document.

You can also change the initial codes style by turning on Reveal Codes (Alt+F3) and double-clicking the [Open Style:InitialStyle] code.

You can define an initial font to override a font in the initial codes style. (See the Initial Font entry.)

Formatting codes entered into the document itself override all initial codes style and initial font settings.

You can also use templates to predefine the look of a document and to determine WordPerfect's behavior and available features. See the Template entry for more information.

If you want to update the Initial Codes Style for use in other documents, use the Styles feature (see the Styles entry). You can update the system style named "InitialStyle" and save your changes to the document template, supplemental template, or a style library file.

 SEE ALSO   *Codes, Font, Initial Font, Styles, Template*

INITIAL FONT

The initial font for a document overrides any font specified in the initial codes style (see the Initial Codes Style entry).

To Choose an Initial Font

1. Choose Layout ➤ Document ➤ Initial Font, or press F9 and choose Initial Font.

2. Choose the font face, font style, and font size as appropriate.

3. Optionally, select the Set As Printer Initial Font checkbox.

4. Choose OK.

 NOTES   Font changes that you make within your document will override the initial font and the initial codes style.

 SEE ALSO   *Font, Font Setup, Initial Codes Style*

INSERT/TYPEOVER

In Insert mode, new text, blank lines, and most codes you type are inserted into existing text at the cursor position. In Typeover mode, new text replaces existing text, but codes are left intact. Press the Insert key to switch between modes.

To Insert Text

In general, follow these steps to insert text or a formatting code:

1. Move the cursor where text should appear or the code should take effect, or select a block of text.

2. Type the text, or insert the code using the pull-down menus or keyboard shortcuts.

NOTES In Typeover mode, pressing Backspace deletes existing text and replaces it with blank spaces (one space for each press of the key). You can press Ctrl+Shift+Z to undelete the text.

Here are some more details about Insert mode:

- If you don't select text before typing, *new text or unpaired codes* will appear at the cursor position.

- If you select text before typing, new text will replace the selected text.

- If you select text before choosing a formatting code, you'll insert paired codes around the selected text.

- To insert blank lines into existing text, move the cursor to the left edge of the line that should appear below the blank lines (or move it to the end of the line that should appear above the blank lines). Press ↵ once for each line you want to insert.

- To insert a blank line as you type, press ↵ twice at the end of the line. (Continue pressing ↵ to add more blank lines.)

- To insert paired formatting codes as you type, choose the pull-down menu option for the paired code or press its shortcut key, and then type the text. To move beyond the paired codes, press →, choose the menu option, or press the shortcut key again.

- To insert characters from the WordPerfect character sets, choose Insert ➤ Character or press Ctrl+W.

- To insert special formatting codes (hard tabs, hard tabs with dot leaders, hyphenation codes, hard spaces, and End Centering/Alignment codes), choose Layout ➤ Line ➤ Other Codes, select the code you want, then choose Insert. Shortcut keys are also available for most of these codes.

- To insert bullets and numbers followed by an indent, choose Insert ➤ Bullets & Numbers or press Ctrl+Shift+B.

👁 **SEE ALSO**   *Bullets and Numbers, Characters, Cursor, Document Window, Font, Hyphenation, Macros, Selecting Text, Spaces (Hard and Soft), Tabs, Undelete*

INSTALL

You must install WordPerfect for Windows before you can use it.

To Install WordPerfect for Windows

1. Start Windows in the usual manner (type <u>win</u> and press ↵ at the DOS prompt).

2. Insert the WordPerfect for Windows disk labeled "Install 1" in drive A or drive B (depending on the size of the diskettes).

3. Choose File ➤ Run from the Program Manager menus.

4. Type *a:\install* (if the Install 1 disk is in drive A) or *b:\install* (if the Install 1 disk is in drive B).

5. Choose OK to start the installation program.

6. Type your Name and License Number into the Registration Information dialog box, then choose Continue.

7. In the Installation Type dialog box, choose the type of installation you want (see Options, below).

8. Choose buttons and fill in dialog boxes according to the options you chose in step 7.

9. To start the installation, choose Start Installation or OK (depending on your choice in step 7). To cancel the installation, choose Close.

10. If you chose to start the installation, feed in new disks and provide other information when prompted.

11. Choose Yes to view the Read Me files or No to bypass them. Then choose OK in the dialog box that tells you WordPerfect has been installed successfully.

To Start WordPerfect for Windows

1. Start Windows if you haven't done so yet.

2. Install the program if you haven't done so yet.

3. Double-click the Program Manager icon (if it's minimized).

4. Double-click the WPWin 6.0 group window icon (if it's minimized).

5. Double-click the WPWin 6.0 icon in the WPWin 6.0 group window.

OPTIONS   You'll find the following installation options in the Installation Type dialog box:

Standard Installs all WordPerfect for Windows files to a hard drive. Requires about 33 MB of disk space.

Custom Lets you choose the source and destination for the WordPerfect for Windows files, which files to install, and which printer drivers to install. It also lets you read the Read Me files, which contain late-breaking news and product information that didn't make it into the WordPerfect manuals.

Network Installs WordPerfect for Windows for use on a network server or workstation.

Minimum Installs a small WordPerfect system (about 11 MB), which doesn't include Speller, Thesaurus, QuickFinder, WP Draw, macros, graphic files, learning files, help files, and other nonessential files. This is helpful if you're short on hard disk space. If more space becomes available later, you can use the Custom installation to add the missing modules.

Options Installs updated printer driver utilities, language modules, and fonts.

 SEE ALSO *Your WordPerfect 6.0 for Windows Manual*

JUSTIFICATION

Justification aligns text between margins. You can justify all text, selected text, or a single line.

To Justify All or Selected Text

1. Move the cursor where the new setting should take effect, or select a block of text.

2. Choose an option from the Layout ➤ Justification menu, press the equivalent shortcut key, or select options from the Justification button on the power bar. (See Options, below.)

To Center or Right-Justify a Single Line

1. Position the cursor at the start of an existing line or where you're about to type a new line.

2. Choose Layout ➤ Line, then either Center or Flush Right. Or press Shift+F7 (Center) or Alt+F7 (Flush Right). To insert a dot leader in front of centered or right-aligned text, repeat this step.

3. If necessary, type the line and press ↵. (Pressing ↵ turns off justification for the line.)

OPTIONS You can choose the following justification options from the Layout ➤ Justification menu or the power bar's Justification button:

Left (Ctrl+L) Aligns text against the left margin, leaving the right margin ragged (uneven).

Right (Ctrl+R) Aligns text against the right margin, leaving the left margin ragged.

Center (Ctrl+E) Centers text between margins.

Full (Ctrl+J) Aligns text evenly against both the left and right margins. WordPerfect expands or compresses spaces between words to even out the line, according to the Word Spacing Justification Limits. (See the Typesetting entry.)

All Similar to Full justification. However, this option also spreads short lines of text to touch the right margin.

NOTES Document justification is ignored in tables. The position of the table on the page is determined by the options in the Alignment area of the Table's Format dialog box (Table ➤ Format or Ctrl+F12)

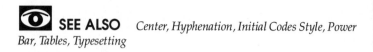 **SEE ALSO**   *Center, Hyphenation, Initial Codes Style, Power Bar, Tables, Typesetting*

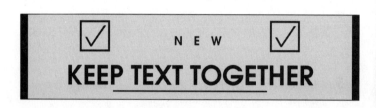

This feature offers three ways to keep your text together—Widow/Orphan, Block Protect, and Conditional End of Page. Use it to prevent text separation across page breaks, to activate widow and orphan protection at first and last lines of paragraphs, and to keep a specific number of lines together.

To Keep Text Together

1. Position the cursor or select the text as follows:

   • For widow/orphan protection or conditional end of page, position the cursor where you want the feature to take effect.

   • For block protection, select the text you want to keep together.

2. Choose Layout ➤ Page ➤ Keep Text Together.

3. To turn a feature on, select (check) it in the dialog box. To turn the feature off, deselect it.

4. If you selected Conditional End of Page in step 3, specify the number of lines you want to keep together. Be sure to include lines of text and any blank lines in between.

5. Choose OK or press ⏎.

NOTES Block protect prevents a passage of text, such as a quotation, sidebar, or columnar table, from being split across two pages. Block protect places paired [Block Pro] codes around a protected block of text. Any changes that you make to the protected block, including new or deleted lines, will still keep the entire block protected.

SEE ALSO *Selecting Text*

KERNING

The process of adjusting the white space between pairs of letters automatically or manually is called *kerning*.

To Kern Letters Automatically

1. Move the cursor to where automatic kerning should start (or end), or select a block of text.

2. Choose Layout ➤ Typesetting ➤ Word/Letterspacing.

3. To turn automatic kerning on, select (check) Automatic Kerning. To turn it off, deselect the option.

4. Choose OK.

To Kern Letters Manually

1. Move the cursor between the two letters you wish to adjust.

2. Choose Layout ➤ Typesetting ➤ Manual Kerning. If necessary, move the Manual Kerning dialog box so that you can see the letters as you're kerning.

3. Optionally, use the Units of Measure drop-down list button to select a unit of measure.

4. In the Amount text box, use the spin buttons to increase or decrease the amount of space between the letters. (With each click of a spin button, the letters will move in the document window.)

5. Choose OK.

 SEE ALSO *Typesetting*

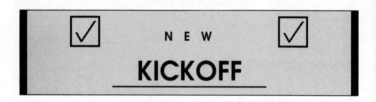

KickOff is an application that starts any application at a specified start time and at a repeat interval. Although KickOff is specially designed to automate updates to QuickFinder indexes, you can use it to launch any program at a specified time.

To Use KickOff

1. Double-click the Kickoff icon in the WPWin 6 group window in Program Manager. The KickOff dialog box appears.

2. You can do any of these tasks:

   • To *add a new event*, choose Add (see "To Add an Event" below).

- To *change settings for an event,* highlight the event in the Events list and choose Edit (or double-click the event you want to change). Edit the event as desired, then choose OK.

- To *delete an event,* highlight the event in the Events list, choose Remove, then choose Yes to confirm the deletion.

- To *customize* KickOff, choose Setup. Select or deselect the options you want, then choose OK. The Setup options are Start KickOff Minimized, Remove Events Upon Completion, Disable Old Events On Startup, and Write Launch Error To Log File.

3. When you're done using KickOff, choose Close.

To Add an Event

1. Choose Add from the KickOff dialog box.

2. Enter the full command line for the program you want to run, or use the Browse button to locate the program. For example, to run the Windows calendar, you'd type *c:\windows\calendar.exe.*

3. Enter the starting Date for the event.

4. Enter the starting Time and choose the appropriate AM or PM setting.

5. To launch the program at regular intervals, enter the number of Days, or Hrs:Mins (hours and minutes), or both to repeat the launch.

6. To run the application minimized, select (check) Run Minimized.

7. To prevent the program from launching from KickOff, select (check) Disable. (This prevents the program from launching automatically until you clear the check box.)

8. Choose OK.

To Launch QuickFinder from KickOff

Follow the steps above for adding an event (don't check Disable in step 7). Use the following command line in step 2:

c:\wpc20\qfwin20.exe options

Replace *options* with any of the following:

/ra Rebuilds all indexes listed in the QuickFinder Index Names list box.

/r-*long name* Rebuilds only the index specified by *long name*

/ia Updates all indexes with new or modified files

/i-*long name* Updates the index specified by *long name* with new or modified files

To specify more than one index name, separate each name by a comma and a space, as in

c:\wpc20\qfwin20.exe /r-document, customer

 SEE ALSO *QuickFinder*

This feature makes it easy to set up and print mailing labels, file folder labels, diskette labels, and index cards.

To Select a Label Format

1. If necessary, choose File ➤ Select Printer and select the printer that you want to use with the labels. Return to the document window.

2. Move the cursor to where the new setting should take effect, or select a block of text.

3. Choose Layout ➤ Labels. The Labels dialog box opens.

4. Optionally, choose Change to select a different file of label formats.

5. Optionally, choose Laser, Tractor-Fed, or Both to select which label formats appear in the list of available labels.

6. In the Labels list, click on or scroll to the label format you want, or type the first few letters of the label type. When you highlight a label, the Label Details area and the sample labels in the dialog box will reflect your current selection. (If the label format you need isn't available, create it yourself, as described below.)

7. When you find the format you want, double-click the format or highlight it and choose Select.

To Type Text for Labels

1. Select a label format as described above.

2. Type each line in the label, pressing ↵ between lines.

3. To start the next label, press Ctrl+↵.

4. Repeat steps 2 and 3 as needed.

To Create, Edit, or Delete a Label Format

1. Optionally, choose File ➤ Select Printer to select the printer you'll be using to print the labels. Return to the document window.

2. Optionally, place the cursor where you want the new label size to take effect.

3. Choose Layout ➤ Labels. The Labels dialog box opens.

4. Choose one of the options below:

- To *create* a new label format, choose Create.

- To *edit* a label format, highlight it in the Labels list and choose Edit.

- To *delete* a label format, highlight it in the Labels list and choose Delete, then choose Yes. Skip to step 6.

5. Fill in the Create Labels or Edit Labels dialog box (see Options, below). Choose OK when done.

6. Choose Cancel to exit the dialog box without selecting a label format, or highlight the format you want and choose Select to select a label format.

OPTIONS These options are available in the Create Labels (or Edit Labels) dialog box. As you make changes, the sample label page at the lower-right corner of the dialog box will reflect your latest choices.

Label Description A unique description for the label.

Label Type Determines which list or lists will display your new format in the Labels dialog box. (Choose Laser, Tractor-Fed, or Both.)

Change Lets you select a paper size.

Label Size Lets you specify the Width and Height of a single label.

Labels Per Page   Lets you specify the number of Columns and Rows in each sheet of labels.

Top Left Label   Lets you define the location of the first label. Specify the Top Edge and Left Edge.

Distance Between Labels   Lets you define the distance between labels. For Columns, type the distance between columns (the physical space between adjacent labels). For Rows, type in the distance between two rows.

Label Margins   Lets you specify the Left, Right, Top, and Bottom margins for a single label.

 NOTES   You can merge information from a merge data file onto labels. Simply select a mailing label format at the top of the form file and perform the merge as usual. (See the Merge Operations entry.)

SEE ALSO   *Envelope, Merge Operations, Paper Size*

LANGUAGE

The Language feature allows you to choose among optional foreign language modules that offer various language-dependent features.

To Choose a Different Language

1. Move the cursor where the new setting should take effect, or select a block of text.

2. Choose Tools ➤ Language.

3. Select the language from the displayed Current Language list, or type the first few letters of the language name.

4. Choose OK.

To Disable or Enable the Writing Tools

1.   Repeat steps 1 and 2 of the previous procedure.

2.   To disable the tools, select (check) Disable Writing Tools (In This Portion Of The Text). To enable the tools, deselect the option.

3.   Choose OK.

NOTES   The currently selected language determines which Speller, Thesaurus, Grammatik, and Hyphenation files WordPerfect will use; the sort order for Sort features; and the language used to display date text and "(continued…)" messages in footnotes.

You can control text for certain features (such as month names) in various languages by editing the WP.LRS language resource file.

SEE ALSO   *Grammatik, Hyphenation, Inital Codes Style, Speller, Thesaurus*

LINE HEIGHT

Line height is the distance between the baseline of one line and the baseline of the next.

To Set Line Height

1.   Move the cursor where the new setting should take effect, or select a block of text.

2.   Choose Layout ➤ Line ➤ Height.

3.   Choose either Auto or Fixed.

4.   If you chose Fixed, press Tab and enter a line height measurement.

5.   Choose OK.

NOTES   If you choose Auto (the default), WordPerfect adds 2 points of space to proportionally spaced fonts and automatically adjusts line height to match the space required for the largest font on a line.

If you choose Fixed, lines will have the height you specify and be evenly spaced, regardless of the font size. Fixed line heights are often used with baseline placement for typesetting (see the Typesetting entry).

Setting the line height has no effect on printers that can print only six lines per inch.

To specify the amount of white space that appears between paragraphs, choose Layout ➤ Paragraph ➤ Format ➤ Spacing Between Paragraphs (see the Paragraph entry).

SEE ALSO   *Font, Initial Codes Style, Line Spacing, Paragraph, Typesetting*

LINE NUMBERING

WordPerfect lets you display and print line numbers on a document. You can change the numbering scheme and position of the number on the line.

To Turn Line Numbering On or Off

1.   Move the cursor to where the new setting should take effect, or select a block of text.

2. Choose Layout ➤ Line ➤ Numbering.

3. To turn line numbering on, select (check) Turn Line Numbering On and continue with step 4. To turn line numbering off, deselect the option and continue with step 5.

4. Adjust the line numbering options, position, and other aspects of the line number appearance if you wish (see Options, below).

5. Choose OK.

OPTIONS   The line numbering options are as follows:

Font Lets you choose the font for line numbers. Make your selections and choose OK.

Numbering Method Lets you choose a numbering method for line numbers. Your options are Number (default), Lowercase Letter, Uppercase Letter, Lowercase Roman, and Uppercase Roman.

Starting Line Number Sets the starting number for line numbering (usually 1).

First Printing Line Number Sets the first line number actually printed (usually 1).

Numbering Interval Numbers only every nth line; enter a number (e.g., 5 will number every fifth line).

From Left Edge Of Page Moves line numbers a specified distance from the left edge of the paper or the center of the space between columns. Select this option, press Tab, then enter a measurement. This option is the default.

Left Of Margin Moves line numbers a specified distance from the left edge of the margin. Select this option, press Tab, then enter a measurement.

Restart Numbering On Each Page When selected, starts line numbers with 1 at the beginning of a new page. When deselected, lines are numbered continuously through the document.

Number All Newspaper Columns   When selected (checked), WordPerfect numbers lines in newspaper columns. Left of Margin is selected automatically and the position setting is reduced.

Count Blank Lines   Select (check) this option to count blank lines. Deselect this option to prevent WordPerfect from numbering or counting blank lines.

NOTES   Headers, footers, and blank lines created by your choices for line spacing are not counted in line numbers.

To add a vertical separator line between the line numbers and the text, choose Graphics ➤ Vertical Line (or press Ctrl+Shift+F11).

SEE ALSO   *Font; Graphic Lines; Headers, Footers, and Watermarks; Initial Codes Style*

LINE SPACING

Line spacing determines the number of lines that will be inserted after each soft return [SRt] or hard return [HRt] code. Single spacing is the default.

To Set Line Spacing

1. Move the cursor to where the new setting should take effect, or select a block of text.

2. Choose Layout ➤ Line ➤ Spacing.

3. Enter the line spacing you want (in whole numbers or fractions) and choose OK.

NOTES   The value you set for line spacing is multiplied by the line height to determine the actual distance between lines (e.g., if line spacing is 2.5 and line height is 0.5", lines will be printed 1.25" apart, baseline to baseline).

You can also use the Line Spacing button on the power bar to change line spacing.

SEE ALSO   *Initial Codes Style, Line Height, Power Bar, Typesetting*

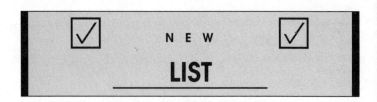

The List feature generates automatic lists of tables, figures, maps, illustrations, or anything else you want. This involves three steps:

1.   Mark items (see below) and assign them to a list. You don't need to mark captions for graphic boxes.

2.   Define the list's location, appearance, and whether it contains graphic box captions.

3.   Generate the lists.

List features are available when the List feature bar is visible.

To Display or Close the List Feature Bar

- To display the feature bar, choose Tools ➤ List

- To hide the feature bar, choose the Close button in the feature bar.

To Mark a List Item

1. Display the List feature bar.

2. Select the text, including any codes that should appear in the list.

3. Click the List drop-down button and type in or choose a list name for the selected text.

4. Choose Mark.

Repeat steps 2–4 for each item you want to mark.

To Define a List

1. Move the cursor to the location where you want the list to appear.

2. Display the List feature bar.

3. Click the Define button in the feature bar.

4. Create a new list or retrieve lists from an existing file.

- To create a new list, click Create, type a unique name for the list, and choose OK. Optionally, select items from Numbering Format, Current Style, and Auto Reference Box Captions to change the numbering format for page numbers, the list style, and referencing of graphics box captions. Choose OK. (See Options, below.)

- To retrieve a list from a file, click Retrieve. In the File-name text box, type the file name that contains the lists you want, or use the file button to locate the file. Choose OK. Select (check) the lists you want to retrieve and choose OK again.

5. Highlight the list you want to insert into the document and choose Insert or press ↵ (or double-click the list name.)

Be sure to define and insert separate lists for each type of graphics box caption you want to track.

Be sure to define and insert separate lists for each type of graphics box caption you want to track.

To Generate a List

1.   Display the List feature bar.

2.   Click the Generate button in the feature bar.

3.   Choose OK.

OPTIONS   You can use these options in the Create List (or Edit List) dialog box to control the appearance of list entries.

Position   Lets you define where the page number appears with respect to the text of the index entry.

Page Numbering   Lets you define the format of the page number.

Change   Lets you change the style of the list entries.

Auto Reference Box Captions   Lets you automatically create a list of graphics box captions for a specified type of graphics box.

NOTES   You can create lists for an individual document or for a master document. Place the list definition in the master document, *not* in a subdocument.

Generated list items will be in the order in which they appear in the document.

To delete a list item, turn on Reveal Codes (Alt+F3) and delete the appropriate [Mrk Txt List] code. Then regenerate the list.

SEE ALSO   *Cross-Reference, Generate, Graphics and Graphics Boxes, Index, Master Document, Page Numbering, Table of Authorities, Table of Contents*

MACROS

Macros let you record the sequences of keystrokes and mouse selections that perform a certain task. You can then "play back" (run or execute) those commands later.

The WordPerfect macro language is a full-featured programming language that lets you write complex macros and interact with the user. You can use the Macros button bar to access most macro features quickly.

To Display the Macros Button Bar

1. If no button bar is visible, choose View ➤ Button Bar.

2. Right-click the button bar and choose Macros from the QuickMenu.

To Record a Macro

1. Choose Tools ➤ Macro ➤ Record, press Ctrl+F10, or click the Macro Record button on the Macros button bar.

2. Optionally, click the Location button on the Record Macro dialog box and select a location for the macro (see Options, below), then choose OK.

3. Choose a name for your macro, if necessary:

- For macros stored in a template, type a unique name (up to 31 characters, including blank spaces).

- For macros stored in a File On Disk, type a valid DOS file name (one to eight characters, no spaces, punctuation, or extension). Or, to create a Ctrl+Shift+*key* macro, press Ctrl and Shift, plus a letter (for example, press Ctrl+Shift+A).

- For macros stored in the Current Document or a New Document, you can't enter a file name now. However,

you *will* need to save the file when you're done recording the macro (see step 8).

4. Choose Record.

5. If the macro already exists, you'll be asked if you want to
replace it. Choose Yes (to overwrite) or No to return to
step 3.

6. The message "Macro Record" appears in the status bar.
Type the keystrokes you want to record, including any
menu choices and shortcuts. (See Notes, below.)

7. To stop recording and save the macro, choose Tools ➤
Macro ➤ Record, press Ctrl+F10, or click the Macro Record button in the Macros button bar. The "Macro Record"
message will disappear from the status bar.

8. If you chose Current Document or New Document in
step 2, macro programming commands will appear in
the document window. Choose Save & Compile from
the Macro Edit feature bar. If prompted, type a valid
DOS file name (one to eight characters, no spaces, punctuation, or extension). Choose Save, then click the Close
button on the feature bar.

To Play a Macro

1. Move the cursor to where you want the macro to start, or
select the text it will act on.

2. If the macro is a Ctrl+Shift+*key* macro, press the Ctrl+Shift
+*key* combination (for example, Ctrl+Shift+A), and the
macro will run.

3. If the macro isn't a Ctrl+Shift+*key* macro, choose Tools ➤
Macro ➤ Play, press Alt+F10, or click the Macro Play button
in the Macros button bar.

4. To choose the location where the macro you want to play
is stored, click the Location button, select the location
(Current Template, Default Template, or File On Disk),
and choose OK.

5. Specify the macro name. For macros stored in a template, highlight or click on the macro name in the Macros In Template list. For macros stored in a File On Disk, type the macro name, or use the file button on the Name text box to locate the macro.

6. Choose Play. The macro will play back your recorded keystrokes.

To Edit a Macro

Macros are stored in standard WordPerfect documents. This makes them easy to edit, format, and print.

1. Choose Tools ➤ Macro ➤ Edit, or click the Macro Edit button in the Macros button bar.

2. If the location is a file on disk, type the file name into the Name text box or use the file button to locate the file. Or, if necessary, choose Location, select your macro's location (Current Template, Default Template, or File On Disk), and choose OK. If the location is a template, highlight the macro you want to edit.

3. Choose Edit.

To Save and Compile a Macro

Whenever you create or edit a macro, WordPerfect *compiles* it once before running it. During compiling, WordPerfect checks for errors and puts the macro into code the computer can understand. Once you're done editing a macro, use any of the following methods to save and compile it.

• To *close the macro editing window,* click Close in the Macro Edit feature bar, then choose Yes if prompted to save changes. WordPerfect will compile the macro if necessary and close the macro editing window and feature bar.

• To *save, compile, and stay* in the macro editing window, click Save & Compile in the feature bar.

- To *save and compile changes in a new macro,* click Save As in the feature bar. Specify a name for your macro and choose Save. You'll remain in the macro editing window, but the new version of the macro you are editing will appear on screen.

To Convert Macros to WordPerfect 6.0 for Windows

To convert a WordPerfect 5.x for Windows or WordPerfect 6.0 for DOS macro to WordPerfect 6.0 for Windows format, follow the steps below:

1. Choose Tools ➤ Macro ➤ Edit command or click the Macro Edit button.

2. Open the macro for editing.

3. Choose Save As from the Macro Edit feature bar, type a valid DOS file name (no extension), and choose Save.

If any commands didn't convert perfectly, error message dialog boxes will tell you what's wrong (click Continue Compilation, or Cancel Compilation to proceed). You'll need to edit and fix the problem commands before you can run the macro.

OPTIONS Many dialog boxes for managing macros have Delete, Location, Menu, and Help buttons.

Delete Lets you delete a macro from a template or the hard disk. Specify the macro you want to delete and click Delete.

Location Lets you choose the location of a macro. Your options include Current Template (the template for the current document file); Default Template (the default template specified in File Preferences); File On Disk (a named file on disk); Current Document (the document you're editing now; useful when adding recorded macro commands to a macro that you're editing); New Document (a new document window); Use as Default (uses the selected location as the default for future macro operations).

Menu Lets you add macros to the Tools ➤ Macro menu. You can add up to ten macros to the menu and can delete unwanted macros from the menu.

Help Provides helpful information about using the macro dialog boxes.

NOTES To play a macro from a menu, choose Tools ➤ Macro and select the macro name. (You must have assigned the macro to the menu. See Options, below and the Preferences entry.)

To play a macro assigned to a button on the Button Bar, click the button. (See the Preferences entry.)

To play a macro assigned to a certain keystroke combination on the keyboard, press that combination. (See the Preferences entry.)

To stop a running macro, press Esc and select OK to remove the macro canceled message from your screen. Then review the document and fix any unwanted changes that the macro made.

For information about macro programming, choose Help ➤ Macros from the WordPerfect menu bar.

Macros stored on disk have the extension .WCM. Macros stored in disk files can be run from *any* WordPerfect document. Macros stored in templates can be run only from documents that use those templates. You can, however, copy macros from one template to another. (See the Template entry.)

Ctrl+Shift+*key* macros offer the quickest way to run a macro. They're stored on disk with names like CTRLSFTA.WCM (for the macro named by pressing Ctrl+Shift+A).

If you record keystrokes in error, you can record the macro again or edit the macro.

When recording a macro, you can use your mouse or keyboard to record any text you type, most editing and cursor movement keys (like ⏎, ↓, ↑, and Backspace), commands you choose, and responses to dialog boxes.

To select text, you must use keyboard techniques such as Shift+arrow or Edit ➤ Select. (See the Selecting Text entry.)

SEE ALSO *Button Bar, Preferences, Template*

If your network has mail software that's compatible with the Microsoft MAPI or Lotus VMI standards, you can use network mail directly from WordPerfect.

See your network administrator for details about what features your network mail program offers.

To Access Network Mail from WordPerfect

1. Sign on to your network.

2. Start Windows and WordPerfect for Windows.

3. Open the document you want to send as a mail message.

4. Choose File ➤ Mail.

5. If necessary, enter your mail user name and password.

6. Use your mail system as required to send, read, and respond to messages.

7. When you're ready to return to WordPerfect, choose an appropriate "close" or "exit" command.

 SEE ALSO *Install*

MARGINS

A margin is the white space between the text and the edge of a printed page. The default margin settings are 1 inch.

To Set Margins

1. Position the cursor where you want the margin changes to start, or select one or more paragraphs of text to limit the changes to those paragraphs.

2. Choose Layout ➤ Margins, press Ctrl+F8, or double-click the top portion of the ruler bar.

3. Enter the measurements for the Left, Right, Top, or Bottom margin.

4. Choose OK.

You can also use the ruler bar to set the left or right margin:

1. Repeat step 1 above.

2. If the ruler isn't visible, choose View ➤ Ruler Bar or press Alt+Shift+F3.

3. Drag the left or right margin marker near the top of the ruler to the margin position you want. As you drag, a dotted vertical line appears and moves to show the changing margin, and the status bar will indicate the current position of the margin.

NOTES To temporarily change the left margin or the left and right margins for the current paragraph, use Indent (F7) or Double Indent (Ctrl+Shift+F7). To temporarily move the left margin back by one tab stop, press Shift+Tab, or choose Layout ➤ Paragraph ➤ Back Tab. (See the Indent entry.)

To adjust margins for future paragraphs or selected paragraphs, use Layout ➤ Paragraph ➤ Format. (See the Paragraph entry.)

👁 **SEE ALSO**   *Binding, Indent, Initial Codes Style, Paragraph, Ruler, Tabs, Typesetting, Units of Measure*

MASTER DOCUMENT

Master documents let you create large documents from smaller, more manageable subdocuments. You can also combine the sub-documents to create indexes, tables of contents, lists, and other addenda for the master document.

To Link a Subdocument to a Master Document

1. Move the cursor to the place in the master document where you want to link the subdocument.

2. Optionally, press Ctrl+↵ to start the subdocument on a new page.

3. Choose File ➤ Master Document ➤ Subdocument.

4. Enter the subdocument file name, or select a file from the displayed list. The subdocument need not exist when you create the link.

5. Click Include. A [subdoc] code appears at the location of the subdocument link.

To Expand a Master Document

Expanding a master document retrieves the existing linked sub-documents into their respective link locations.

1. Choose File ➤ Master Document ➤ Expand Master.

2. Select (check) the subdocuments you want to expand. (You can use the Mark button to Mark All or Clear All check boxes at once.)

3.   Choose OK.

To Condense a Master Document

Condensing a master document removes the linked subdocument text but retains the links:

1.   Choose File ➤ Master Document ➤ Condense Master.

2.   Select (check) the subdocuments you want to condense and the ones you want to save. You only need to save subdocuments that you changed while editing the master document. (You can use the Mark button to Condense All, Clear Condense, Save All, or Clear Save.)

3.   Choose OK.

To Structure
Master Documents and Subdocuments

The master document should be a skeleton structure for your final document. It should contain only the following:

- Formatting codes that apply to *all* subdocuments

- Links to each subdocument

- Titles and definitions for endnote location, tables of authorities, tables of contents, indexes, and lists

Subdocuments should contain everything else needed to build the final document, including:

- Text and graphics for each chapter, section, etc.

- Formatting codes specific to each subdocument

- Marked text for cross-references, footnotes, endnotes, tables of authorities, tables of contents, indexes, and lists

To Generate Lists for Master Documents

You can choose whether to save changes to subdocuments when you generate lists for a master document.

1. Choose Tools ➤ Generate or press Ctrl+F9, then choose Options.

2. Select (check) Save Subdocuments to save the changes; deselect the option to generate the lists without saving changes first (this will be faster).

3. Choose OK twice to start generating the lists.

NOTES Typically, you'll edit the subdocuments separately, then use a master document to assemble them, but you can also edit the text of an expanded master document, including subdocument text.

In draft view, subdocument links appear as comments containing *Subdoc:* followed by the path name of the subdocument. In Page view or Two-Page view, subdocuments appear as icons that you can click to see the subdocument name. In Reveal Codes (Alt+F3), the linked subdocuments are marked by [Subdoc] or [Subdoc Begin] and [Subdoc End] codes.

You must expand a master document before printing, unless you actually want to print the condensed version.

You don't have to expand a master document before generating lists, tables of contents, and similar items.

SEE ALSO *Comment, Cross-Reference, Footnotes and Endnotes, Generate, Index, List, Table of Authorities, Table of Contents*

MENUS

WordPerfect for Windows uses the standard Windows Common User Access (CUA) conventions—pull-down menus, dialog boxes, buttons, and scroll bars—to provide access to its features. This entry discusses the use of pull-down menus and of the available keystroke alternatives to the various elements of the CUA.

To Choose Menu Options

To use the mouse to choose a menu option:

1. Click on the menu name.

2. Move the mouse pointer to the desired option.

3. Click on the option.

4. Repeat steps 2 and 3 to move through any submenus.

To use the keyboard to select a menu option:

• Press the Alt key and press the underlined letter of the menu you want. Then press the underlined letter of the option you want.

Here's another way to select a menu option using the keyboard:

1. Press, then release the Alt key to activate the menu bar.

2. Use the arrow keys to highlight the menu you want to open and press ↵, ↓, or ↑ to reveal the menu. Press ↑ or ↓ to move *within* a menu. Press ← or → to move *across* the menu bar.

3. Press ↵ when the option you want is highlighted.

To Cancel a Menu Choice

• Click the menu name or any empty space outside the menu.

• Press and release Alt, F10, or Esc.

To Use Shortcut Keystrokes

Hold down the first key while pressing the second key. For example, to press Shift+F4, hold down Shift, press F4, and then release both keys.

NOTES Table III describes some of the symbols used on pull-down menus.

Table III: WordPerfect Menu Symbols

SYMBOL	MEANING
… (ellipsis)	Choosing the menu option will take you to a dialog box
Dimmed (grayed)	A dimmed option is currently unavailable
Check mark (✓)	The checked option is currently active ("on")
Triangle (➤)	Leads to another submenu of additional commands
Shortcut key	Indicates a shortcut key (such as F4) or keystroke combination (such as Shift+F4) that you can use instead of choosing menu options

You can set up custom menus of your own, or edit existing menus if they were not predefined by WordPerfect. Choose File ➤ Preferences ➤ and double-click Menu Bar.

👁 **SEE ALSO**   *Cancel, Dialog Boxes, Help, Windows*

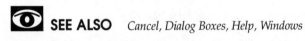

MERGE OPERATIONS

Merge operations combine information from two sources into a single document. For example, you can use merging to print form letters addressed to many different people.

Merging involves three basic operations:

- Creating a data file of variable information (e.g., names and addresses)

- Creating a form file of standard information (e.g., a form letter)

- Merging the two files into a new document. The merge data can also come from the keyboard or an ASCII text file.

To Create a Data File

1. Choose _Tools_ ➤ _Merge_, press Shift+F9, or click the Merge button in the WordPerfect button bar.

2. If you want to place the records in a WordPerfect table, select (check) _Place Records In A Table_.

3. Click the _Data_ button.

4. If there's already information in the current document, you'll be asked if you want to use the current document or open a new one. Select an option and choose OK. The Create Data File dialog box appears.

5. For each _field_ you want to define (see Notes, below), enter a field name (up to 40 characters, including spaces), then choose _Add_ or press ⏎.

- Add field names in the same order that data will be entered.

- If you need to rearrange fields or change field names, click a name in the field list and use the _Replace_, _Delete_, Move _Up_, or Move _Down_ buttons to change the field name or position.

6. When you're done entering field names, choose OK. The Quick Data Entry dialog box will appear.

7. For each _record_ (see Notes, below), type the data and press ⏎ or click Next Field. When you finish typing the last field in a record, pressing ⏎ will automatically start the next record.

8. If necessary, use the buttons in the Quick Data Entry dialog box to move from field to field, add new records, delete records, find records, or edit the field names. When you're done adding data, choose Close.

9. You'll be asked if you want to save your changes. To save your changes now, choose Yes, enter a file name, and choose OK. To skip the save for now, choose No.

10. The Merge feature bar will appear. You can use its buttons to make further changes if you wish (see Options, below).

11. When you're done, choose File ➤ Close, and save your changes if prompted.

To Create a Form File

1. Choose Tools ➤ Merge, press Shift+F9, or click the Merge button in the WordPerfect button bar.

2. Choose Form.

3. If there's already information in the current document, you'll be asked if you want to use the current document or open a new one. Select an option and choose OK.

4. If you want to associate a data file with this form file, select Associate A Data File, and type the data file name and extension (or use the file button to locate the file). If you don't want to associate a data file, choose None. Then choose OK. The Merge feature bar will appear.

5. Place any formatting options you want for the merged document in Initial Codes Style.

6. Type your form file (e.g., type a letter) until you come to a place where you want to insert a field from a data file, a date code, a merge code, or a prompt for data entry from the keyboard.

7. Choose an appropriate button from the Merge feature bar (see Options, below) and fill in any dialog boxes that appear.

8. Repeat steps 6 and 7 until you're done typing the form.

9. Save your changes and close the file (File ➤ Close ➤ Yes).

To Edit a Data or Form File

To edit a data or form file that you've already saved and closed,

1. Open it as you would any normal file (choose File ➤ Open, Ctrl+O, or the Open button on the power bar).

2. Use normal editing techniques and the buttons on the Merge feature bar to make your changes (see Options, below). Be careful not to delete any merge commands or page breaks unless you know what they're for.

3. Save your changes and close the file (File ➤ Close ➤ Yes).

To Perform a Merge

1. Choose Tools ➤ Merge, press Shift+F9, or click the Merge button in the WordPerfect button bar.

2. Choose Merge. The Perform Merge dialog box opens.

3. In the Form File text box, specify the form file or use the button in the text box to select a file on disk, the current document, or the Clipboard.

4. In the Data File text box, specify the data file. You can use the button in the text box to select a file on disk, no document (if all the input is from the keyboard), or the Clipboard.

5. In the Output File text box, specify the output file. You can use the button in the text box to select the current document, new document, printer, or a file on disk.

6. Optionally, choose buttons described below. Fill in the dialog boxes that appear and choose OK until you return to the Perform Merge dialog box.

Select Records Lets you choose which records are included in the merge. You can either specify the conditions for included records (based on field value or record number range) or mark records individually.

Envelopes Lets you format an envelope for each record in the output file.

Options Lets you customize the format of the output file and choose options for keyboard merges.

Reset Returns the Select Records, Envelopes, and Options settings to their previous values.

7. When you're ready to perform the merge, choose OK.

8. If the data file is not a WordPerfect file, the Convert File Format dialog box will open. Select the format you want to convert from and choose OK. For example, you would choose *ANSI Delimited Text (Windows)* for a Microsoft Excel spreadsheet that you saved in "Text" format.

To Change Default Settings for ASCII Delimited Text Files

The data file can contain delimited text format data, such as that exported from spreadsheet and database files. The default field delimiter for a comma separated value (comma delimited) text file is a comma. The record delimiter is a carriage return–linefeed sequence [CR][LF]. Strings of characters are enclosed in double-quotation marks ("). To change the default settings:

1. Choose File ➤ Preferences, double-click Import, change the settings as needed, and choose OK, then Close.

To Interact with a Merge

When defining a form file, you can use the Keyboard button in the Merge feature bar to request input from the user. During the merge, WordPerfect will pause at the KEYBOARD command, display the message you entered as a prompt, and wait for keyboard input. Respond by typing the required data, then choose Continue from the feature bar to continue the merge.

Choose these options from the Feature bar during a keyboard merge.

Continue To continue the merge.

Stop To stop the merge at the cursor position.

Quit To stop the merge after including any remaining text.

Skip Record To skip the current record and go on to the next.

OPTIONS Choose any of these buttons on the Merge feature bar when you create or change a *data file*:

Row (Table data files only.) Lets you insert or delete a row (record) in the table.

Column (Table data files only.) Lets you insert or delete a column (field name) in the table.

End Field (Non-table data files only.) Ends the data field at the cursor position. You can also press Alt+↵ to end a field.

End Record (Non-table data files only.) Ends the data record at the cursor position. You can also press Alt+Shift+↵ to end a record.

Merge Codes Lets you insert merge codes (commands) from the Insert Merge Codes list. To select a code, highlight it in the Insert Merge Codes dialog box and choose Insert, or double-click the code. To highlight a code quickly, type the first few letters of its name.

Quick Entry Goes to the Quick Data Entry dialog box, which makes it easy to enter records. See "To Create a Data File" (steps 7–10) above for details.

Merge Opens the Merge dialog box. (Same as choosing Tools ➤ Merge, pressing Alt+F9, or clicking the Merge button in the WordPerfect button bar.)

Go To Form Lets you switch to a form file. If no form file is currently associated with the data file, you'll be asked to select or create one.

Options Lets you sort or print the data file, control the appearance of merge codes, and remove the Merge feature bar.

Choose any of these buttons on the Merge feature bar when you create or change a *form file*:

Insert Field Inserts a field name and code at the cursor position. Choose Insert Field to open the Insert Field Name Or Number dialog box. You can double-click a field name in the Field Names list (or highlight it and choose Insert). If the Field

Names list is empty, or you want to insert fields from a different data file, choose <u>D</u>ata File, select the file you want, and choose OK.

Date Inserts a DATE code at the cursor position. During a merge, this code will be replaced by the system date.

Merge Codes Same as the Merge Codes button for data files, described above.

Keyboard Inserts a KEYBOARD code at the cursor position. Choose <u>K</u>eyboard, enter the prompt you want to display during a merge, and choose OK. During a merge, WordPerfect will pause at the KEYBOARD code and let the user enter data.

Merge Same as Merge button for data files, described above.

Go To Data Lets you switch to a data file. If no data file is currently associated with the form file, you'll be asked to select or create one.

Options Lets you control the appearance of merge codes and remove the Merge feature bar.

NOTES Each complete piece of information in the data file is called a *record,* and each record is divided into one or more *fields.* For example, a customer record might include the fields *Last Name, First Name, Middle Initial, Street Address, City, State, Zip Code,* and so on.

The *data file* contains the data to be inserted into the form file. Data files can contain many records separated by merge codes or arranged in a table. It's usually easier to enter data if you store it as a table.

Table data files can have up to 64 columns (fields). Non-tabular data files can have up to 255 fields.

Data files also can come from the keyboard or an ASCII delimited text file. (Many database, spreadsheet, and word processing programs can create ASCII delimited text files.)

Before merging, you can sort the data file or select records from it. (See Options (above) and the Sorting and Selecting entry.)

A *form file* contains standard text, graphics, and formatting information; field names indicating where to insert data from the data file; and, optionally, other merge commands.

The form file can insert and reuse fields from the data file in any order. It need not use every field in the data file.

During a merge, information from the data file, keyboard, or delimited text file is substituted into the appropriate fields of the form file, and the file is formatted automatically.

SEE ALSO   *Envelope, Find, Initial Codes Style, Preferences, Sorting and Selecting, Tables*

MOUSE

The mouse makes it easy to navigate the WordPerfect for Windows graphical user interface. Most mouse operations in WordPerfect are the same ones used in other Windows applications.

To Use Your Mouse

Here are some commonly-used mouse terms:

Click: Press the left button and release immediately.

Double-click: Click the left button two times quickly.

Drag: Press the left button and hold it down while moving the mouse. Release the mouse button when you're done.

Right-click: Click the right button.

To Select Text

To select text for cutting and pasting, changing fonts, or other operations:

1.   Position the cursor at the start of the text.

2.   Press and hold down the left mouse button.

3.   Drag the mouse pointer to the end of the text. The text the mouse pointer passes over will be highlighted.

4.   Release the mouse button.

To deselect the text, click the left mouse button again.

To select a word, double-click it. To select a sentence, triple-click it. To select a paragraph, quadruple-click it. Or move the pointer to the left margin (the pointer changes to an arrow) and click once to select a sentence or twice to select a paragraph. Or, move the pointer to the left margin, right-click, and choose "Select ..." options from the QuickMenu.

To Choose Menu and Dialog Box Options

- To choose menu options, click on the menu name, then click on the item you want. Or click on the menu name, drag the mouse to the item you want, then release the button.

- To select an item from a list box and take the default action, double-click the item. Or click the item and choose the default button (the one with the dark outline).

- To turn a check box item on or off, move the mouse pointer to the square and click the mouse button.

- To select a radio button, click it.

To Use Graphics Boxes

- To select a graphics box, click anywhere in the box. To deselect it, click outside the box.

- To move a graphics box, select the box and drag it to the new location. The mouse pointer appears as a four-headed arrow when you can move the box.

- To size a box, select the box, then drag one of the square handles along the box border to achieve the desired size. The mouse appears as a two-headed arrow when you can size the box.

- To open the editor for the graphics box, double-click any-where in the box.

To Open a QuickMenu

- Right-click a "hot spot" on the screen. Then click the left or right mouse button on the option you want. (See the QuickMenu entry.)

To Open a Dialog Box from Reveal Codes

- Turn on Reveal Codes (Alt+F3) and double-click the code for the feature you want to change. The dialog box for that feature will open. (This works for many codes.)

NOTES Before using the mouse, you must install it as explained in your documentation and then set up the mouse for use with Windows. Customize your mouse's behavior through the Windows Control Panel.

Always click the left mouse button, unless otherwise directed (or unless you have switched the left and right button functions).

Whenever you move the mouse pointer to a button in the button bar, power bar, feature bar, or status bar, WordPerfect will display a short message in the title bar about what that button does.

SEE ALSO *Dialog Boxes, Graphics and Graphics Boxes, Menus, QuickMenu, Reveal Codes, Selecting Text*

NEW

You can open a new blank document window at any time (up to a limit of nine documents).

To Open a New Document Window

- Choose File ➤ New, press Ctrl+N, or click the New Document button in the power bar.

To Open a New
Document Window with Any Template

- Choose File ➤ Template (Ctrl+T), select a template, and choose OK.

You also can edit and create templates if you wish. (See the Template entry.)

👁 **SEE ALSO**   *Open, Power Bar, Preferences, Save/Save As, Template*

OBJECT LINKING AND EMBEDDING

You can use object linking and embedding (OLE) to link or embed graphics images, text, charts, spreadsheets, sound clips, video clips, and other Windows objects in a WordPerfect document or another application. For linked objects, if the source object changes in WordPerfect or the application that created the object, the object will be updated automatically in both places. (See your Windows documentation for more details on this topic.)

WordPerfect offers three ways to link or embed objects:

- Insert ➤ Object (described below)

- Edit ➤ Paste Special ➤ Paste Link (described below)

- Insert ➤ Spreadsheet/Database (see the Spreadsheet/Database Import and Link entry).

To Embed an Object

1. Choose Insert ➤ Object.

2. Highlight the Object Type you want and choose OK (or double-click your choice). The server application for the object will open.

3. Create the object (Paintbrush picture, spreadsheet, etc.).

4. Choose File ➤ Update to embed the object if you want to remain in the server application.

5. To return to WordPerfect, choose File ➤ Exit. The embedded object will appear in a graphics box in your document.

To Paste Link an Object

1. While WordPerfect is running, switch to Program Manager (Ctrl+Esc or Alt+Tab).

2. Open the server application for the object you want to paste link into your WordPerfect document.

3. In the server application, create and save the file you want to paste link, or open an existing file.The server file must be saved.

4. Select the object or portion of the object you want to link, then cut or copy the selection to the Clipboard.

5. Switch back to WordPerfect (Ctrl+Esc or Alt+Tab).

6. Position the cursor where you want the object to appear.

7. Choose Edit ➤ Paste Special.

8. Highlight the Data Type of the object you want to paste link. (For example, to paste link a Paintbrush object, highlight PBrush Object.) The Paste Link button will stay gray until you choose an object type that can be paste linked.

9. Choose Paste Link. The linked object will appear in a graphics box.

10. Optionally, switch back to the server application and exit the application (File ➤ Exit) You must save the server file first so the links will be saved.

To View, Edit, or Play Back a Linked or Embedded Object

1. Double-click the object. Or select (click on) the object, then choose Edit ➤ ...Object from the WordPerfect menus or right-click and choose ...Object from the QuickMenu.

2. For some objects (such as sound files), Edit ➤ ... Object will offer additional menu selections. Choose the one you want.

3. If you chose an "edit" option, make your changes. When you're done, choose File ➤ Exit ➤ Yes to update the object in WordPerfect.

To Edit a Link

To update, cancel, or change links to paste linked objects:

1. Choose Edit ➤ Links.

2. Highlight the link you want to update, then do one of the following:

- To link to a different file name, choose Change Link and double-click the file you want (or highlight it and choose OK).

- To update the link with any recent changes, choose Update Now.

- To change the link type, choose Automatic or Manual. Automatic links are updated whenever the file changes. Manual links are updated only when you choose Update Now.

- To break the link, choose Cancel Link. The object will remain in the document. However, it will no longer be linked to the source file or application.

NOTES   Upon opening a document that contains links to other files, you'll be asked for permission to update the links. Choose Yes to update the links, or No to skip the updates.

You can use normal copy and paste procedures to paste text or graphics from a WordPerfect document into another Windows application. For example, to paste a graphic from WordPerfect into a Paintbrush document, select the graphic in WordPerfect and choose Edit ➤ Copy (Ctrl+C). Open or switch to Paintbrush, then choose Edit ➤ Paste (Ctrl+V) from the application's menus.

SEE ALSO   *Graphics and Graphics Boxes, Spreadsheet/Database Import and Link*

OPEN

Use the Open feature to open and manage files. The Open File dialog box and other similar dialog boxes use standard Windows techniques for navigating the DOS file system.

To Open a Recently-Saved Document

1. Choose File from the menu bar.

2. If the file you want to open is at the bottom of the File menu, click its name. If it is not, see "To Open Any Document" below. Only the last four files you opened are listed.

To Open Any Document

1. Choose File ➤ Open, press Ctrl+O or F4, or click the Open button in the power bar. The Open File dialog box appears.

2. In the Filename text box, type the name of the file exactly as you typed it when you first saved it (e.g., **myfirst.wpd**) and choose OK; or type the full drive, directory, and file name (e.g, **c:\wpwin60\wpdocs\myfirst.wpd**) and choose OK; or double-click the file name in the Filename list.

To Search for and Open a Document

If the file you're looking for is on another drive and/or directory, you can search for it and then open it.

1. Go to the Open File dialog box (step 1 above).

2. The list below the Filename text box initially shows all files in the current directory that have a .WPD extension. To list a different group of file names, use any of the methods below:

- If the file is on a different drive, choose the drive you want from the Drives drop-down list.

- If the file is on a different directory, choose the directory you want from the Directories list. (For example, double-click the directory you want or highlight it and press ↵.)

- To list files of a different type, select List Files Of Type and select a file type from the pull-down list.

- To specify the drive, directory, and file type all at once, type the full path name and wild cards into the File-name text box and choose OK. For example, typing **c:\wpwin60\mydocs\e*.*** into the box would list all files that start with *e* in the \WPWIN60\MYDOCS directory on drive C.

3. When the list shows the file name you want to open:

- Double-click the file name you want, or
- Or, press Tab or Shift+Tab until the outline is in the File-name list. Use the arrow keys to highlight the file you want, or type the first few characters in the file name. Choose OK.

Opening More than One File

You can have up to nine files open at once. To open multiple files, use standard Windows techniques to select multiple items in the Filename list. After selecting the files, choose OK to open them.

OPTIONS   These buttons are available in the Open File dialog box:

View: Opens the Viewer window, which lets you look at most files without opening them first. To see what's in a file, click on it or scroll to it in the Filename list box and look at the Viewer window. You can Maximize, Restore, Move, Size, or Close (Alt+F4) the Viewer window as needed. To search through the file shown in the Viewer, click on the Viewer window and press F2 to open the Find dialog box. (See the Find entry.) You can also scroll through the displayed file with the scrollbars.

QuickFinder: Lets you use the QuickFinder to locate files.

QuickList Lets you edit or display the QuickList or display both the QuickList and Directories.

File Options: Lets you use these file management commands: Copy, Move, Rename, Delete, Change Attributes, Print (a file), Print List (of displayed or selected file names in the dialog box), Create Directory, Remove Directory.

Setup: Lets you   and control the sort order and file name details in the dialog box, create speedup files, and decide whether the default directory changes when you use the Directories list.

Help: Provides help on file management operations.

NOTES The Open File dialog box works like many other WordPerfect for Windows dialog boxes that open or save files. You can also right-click the Filename or directories lists, QuickList, or Viewer window and select QuickMenu options.

SEE ALSO *Combine Documents, Find, New, Power Bar, QuickFinder, QuickList, Save/Save As*

OUTLINE

WordPerfect's Outline feature makes it easy to number paragraphs and create hierarchical outlines. The outline is renumbered automatically as you make changes.

In the discussion below, the term *outline* refers to anything that WordPerfect should number automatically. The term *numbers* refers to numbers, bullets, heading styles, roman numerals, letters, or any other character or appearance change that WordPerfect can display in an outline item.

To Display or Close the Outline Feature Bar

In the Outline feature bar provides everything you need for automatic outlining.

- To display the Outline feature bar, choose Tools ➤ Outline.

- To hide the Outline feature bar, click its Close button.

Refer to Table IV for a complete list of Outline bar buttons and features.

Table IV: The Outline Feature Bar's Features and Buttons

FEATURE	BUTTON	PURPOSE
Feature bar help and options	?	Provides menu options and lists keyboard shortcuts for many outlining features.
Previous level	←	Promotes an outline item to a higher level.
Next level	→	Demotes an outline item to a lower level.
Move up	↑	Moves the current paragraph or selection up without changing its level.
Move down	↓	Moves the current paragraph or selection down without changing its level.
Change to or from body text	T	Converts body text to an outline item; converts an outline item to body text.
Show family	+	Shows all members of an outline family.
Hide family	−	Hides all but the main level of an outline family.
Show level n	**1, 2, 3, 4, 5, 6, 7, 8**	Shows outline level n or higher, where n is the level indicated on the button. Excludes body text.
Show all levels	<u>A</u>ll	Shows all outline levels, including body text.

Table IV: The Outline Feature Bar's Features and Buttons
(continued)

FEATURE	BUTTON	PURPOSE
Outline options	Options	Provides options for defining an outline, marking the end of an outline, inserting a new item at a specified level, and setting the level number of an item.
Outline style	drop-down list	Lets you choose a different outline numbering style from a drop-down list.
Close feature bar	Close	Hides the Outline feature bar.

To Display the Outline Button Bar

The Outline button bar offers many outlining shortcuts. To display it:

1. If no button bar is visible, choose View ➤ Button Bar.

2. Right-click the button bar and select Outline from the QuickMenu.

To Create an Outline

1. Move the cursor to where the outline should begin.

2. Choose one of the methods below to start the outline:

   • If the Outline feature bar isn't visible, choose Tools ➤ Outline. Choose the outline style you want from the

Outline Definitions drop-down list in the Outline feature bar. Skip to step 5 below.

- If the Outline feature bar is already on the screen, click
  the Options button, choose Define Outline, and continue with step 3 below.

- Click the Define Outline button on the Outline button
  bar. Continue with step 3.

- Move the mouse pointer to the left margin of the document window (the pointer changes to an arrow),
  right-click the mouse, and choose Outline from the
  QuickMenu. Continue with step 3.

3.   Select (check) Start New Outline.

4.   In the Name list, highlight the style you want and choose
  OK, or double-click the style name.

5.   To enter text, do one of the following:

- To keep the item at the *current level*, type the text for the
  item. The text can be one line or an entire paragraph.

- To *demote the item* to a lower level, press Tab or click the
  → button in the Outline feature bar once for each level
  you want to move down. (You can have up to eight levels.) Type your line or paragraph of text.

- To *promote the item* to a higher level, press Shift+Tab or
  click the ← button in the Outline feature bar once for
  each level you want to move up. Type your text.

- To *assign the item to a specific level number* (between 1
  and 8), click the Options button in the Outline feature
  bar and select Change Level (or click the Outline Level
  button in the Outline button bar). Type the level number you want and choose OK. Type your text.

6.   After you've finished typing the item, you can enter another numbered item:

- If you're using an *automatic style*, press ↵ to move to the
  next item and insert the next numbering character (or
  style) at the current outline level. You can press ↵ more

than once to add blank lines between items and move the outline number down.

- If you're using a *manual style*, press ↵ (as many times as you want), then click the T button in the Outline feature bar. An outline numbering character (or style) will appear.

- To turn off automatic numbering temporarily, click the T button in the Outline feature bar. To turn the numbering on again, click the T button again.

7. Repeat steps 5 and 6 as needed.

8. To turn off outline numbering, click the Options button and choose End Outline (or click the End Outline Button in the Outline button bar). (If a leftover outline number appears above the cursor, press Backspace as many times as needed to remove it.)

To Change an Outline

1. Move the cursor to the item you want to change. Or, if you want to change some feature that affects the entire outline (such as the outline style), move the cursor anywhere in the outline.

2. Click a button in the Outline feature bar (see Table IV, above).

To Use the Outline Editor

The outline editing tools appear at the left edge of the document window and are visible whenever the Outline feature bar is turned on. The hollow numbers (*level markers*) mark the relative level of each item within the outline. Minus (–) signs symbolize hidden families, plus (+) signs indicate fully expanded families, and hollow T symbols (*text markers*) denote body text.

- To *select an outline family*, move the mouse pointer to the highest level marker or text marker that you want to select (the mouse pointer will change to a two-headed vertical arrow), and click the left mouse button. (You can also use the Outline button bar to select outline items. To *select one outline item*, move the cursor to the item and click the Select Paragraph button. To select an outline family, move the cursor to the topmost item in the family and click the Select Family button).

- To *delete an outline family*, select it, then press Delete.

- To *collapse an outline family*, move the cursor to the topmost item that you want to see. Move the mouse pointer to the marker for that item, then double-click. Or, click the - button in the Outline feature bar.

- To *expand an outline family*, repeat the steps given just above for collapsing an outline family.

- To *move an outline family* to a new position in the outline, select the family. Move the mouse pointer to the topmost level marker in the family and drag the marker to its new position. As you drag the marker, a horizontal bar will indicate the new position of the family. When you release the mouse button, the family will appear at the new position and the outline will be renumbered automatically. As an alternative to dragging, you can select the family, then click ↑ and ↓ in the Outline feature bar until you've placed the family where you want it.

- To *copy an outline family* to a new position in the outline, collapse the family (if you wish), select it, then choose Edit ➤ Copy (Ctrl+C). Click in the outline where you want to place the copied family, then press Home twice and choose Edit ➤ Paste (Ctrl+V).

- To undo editing mistakes (if you catch the mistake immediately), choose Edit ➤ Undo (Ctrl+Z).

NOTES The numbered items in an outline are called *outline levels* and the "normal" unnumbered text is *body text*. You can freely mix outline levels with body text in any outline.

150   Overstrike

Most outlines consist of groups of related ideas, with each idea or topic placed on a level by itself. A topic and all of its subtopics compose a *family*.

WordPerfect comes with seven built-in numbering styles. A numbering style can be either automatic or manual. In the *automatic* style, WordPerfect inserts the next item number automatically, as soon as you turn outlining on and whenever you press the ↵ key at the end of a numbered line or paragraph. All the built-in styles, except the *Headings* and *Numbers* styles, are automatic. In the *manual* style, you must tell WordPerfect explicitly when you want to enter another numbered item.

◉ SEE ALSO   *Bullets and Numbers, Button Bar, Characters, Counter, Indent, Initial Codes Style, Styles, Tabs*

OVERSTRIKE

The Overstrike command lets you print two or more characters on top of one another to create special characters not normally available on your printer.

To Create an Overstrike

1. Move the cursor to where you want the overstrike.

2. Choose Layout ➤ Typesetting ➤ Overstrike.

3. In the Overstrike dialog box, click the button to the right of the Characters text box (or press F4) and assign any font attributes you want. Attribute codes will appear in the text box, with the cursor between them.

4. Enter the overstriking characters and choose OK.

To Edit an Overstrike

1. Place the cursor just before or after an existing overstrike combination.

2. Choose Layout ➤ Typesetting ➤ Overstrike.

3. Click the Previous or Next button until you locate the overstrike you want. If you get an "…Overstrike Not Found" message, choose OK to clear it.

4. Edit the overstrike combination. (If you make an editing mistake and want to return to the original overstrike character, choose Reset.)

5. Choose Close.

As a shortcut for steps 1–3 above, you can View Reveal Codes (Alt+F3) and double-click the [Ovrstk] code for the combination you want to change.

 NOTES   Overstruck characters are printed one over the other, without advancing the print head (e.g., 0/ prints a zero with a slash through it, Ø.

Overstrike character combinations available through WordPerfect's character sets should be entered using Ctrl+W key combinations rather than with Overstrike.

SEE ALSO   *Characters, Codes, Font*

PAGE BREAKS

WordPerfect paginates documents automatically by inserting a soft page break code [SPg] when you reach the bottom margin of a page, column, or label. You can control page breaks manually by inserting hard page breaks and keeping specified text together on a page.

To Insert a Hard Page Break

1. Position the cursor where you want the page to break.

2. Press Ctrl+↵ or choose Insert ➤ Page Break.

NOTES   A hard page break is also used to end one column or label and move to the next.

In Draft mode, soft page breaks appear as single horizontal lines across the screen. Hard page breaks appear as double horizontal lines across the page.

To delete hard page break codes [HPg] and codes that keep text together ([Wid/Orph:On], [Block Pro], and [Condl EOP]), turn on Reveal Codes (Alt+F3) and delete the code. (You can't delete soft page breaks.)

SEE ALSO   *Force Page, Keep Text Together, Page Numbering, Selecting Text, Suppress*

PAGE NUMBERING

The page numbering features let you specify the location and appearance of page numbers and insert page numbers within text.

To Start Page Numbering

1. Position the cursor on the page where numbering should begin.

2. Choose Layout ➤ Page ➤ Numbering to open the Page Numbering dialog box.

3. From the Position pop-up list button, choose a location for page numbers: No Page Numbering (default), Top Left, Top Center, Top Right, Alternating Top, Bottom Left, Bottom Center, Bottom Right, or Alternating Bottom.

4. If you wish, choose Options and define the format and accompanying text for page, secondary page, chapter, and volume numbers, then choose OK. (See Notes, below.)

5. Optionally, choose Value and set page number values for page, secondary page, chapter, or volume page numbers, then choose OK.

6. Optionally, choose Font, select from various font options for the page numbers, and choose OK.

7. Choose OK to return to the document.

To Insert a Page Number in Text

1. Position the cursor where you want to insert the page number.

2. Choose Layout ➤ Page ➤ Numbering.

3. Use either method below to insert the page number:

- To insert an unformatted page number, choose Value, then select (check) the Insert And Display At Insertion Point option for the type of page number you want to insert. (See Notes, below.)

- To insert the formatted page number, choose Options and select Insert Format And Accompanying Text At Insertion Point.

4. Choose OK twice, or choose OK and Close.

As a shortcut for inserting the formatted page number, you can press Ctrl+Shift+P.

To Include Page Numbers in Headers or Footers

- Click the Number button in the header/footer feature bar and choose a page number option.

To Format the Page Numbers

Choose Options in the Page Numbering dialog box if you want to customize the page number format:

- You can choose a numbering method from the Page, Secondary, Chapter, or Volume pop-up list buttons. The numbering methods are Numbers, Lowercase Letter, Uppercase Letter, Lowercase Roman, and Uppercase Roman.

- You can use the Format And Accompanying Text box to format the page number text. Type any text you want to appear. When you want to insert a page numbering placeholder, click Insert and select Page Number, Secondary Number, Chapter Number, or Volume Number.

NOTES Document pages are numbered only if you request it. Page numbers will appear in Page view or Two-Page view and in the printed document. Use the Suppress command to prevent page numbers from printing on a certain page (for example, a title page) without interrupting the numbering sequence.

You can have four levels of page numbers: page number, secondary (section) number, chapter number, and volume number. WordPerfect increments the page and secondary numbers automatically. Chapter and volume page numbers stay the same unless you change them manually.

👁 **SEE ALSO**   *Font; Headers, Footers, and Watermarks; Initial Codes Style; Suppress; View*

PAPER SIZE

Use the Paper Size feature to select from the extensive list of Word-Perfect's predefined paper sizes or to create non-standard paper sizes for documents such as labels and envelopes.

To Select, Create, Edit, or Delete a Paper Size

1. Position the cursor where the paper size should take effect.

2. Select the printer you want to use (File ➤ Select Printer) and return to the document window.

3. Choose Layout ➤ Page ➤ Paper Size to open the Paper Size dialog box.

4. If you want to select, edit, or delete a paper size, highlight the paper size you want.

5. Choose one of these options:

- To *select* the highlighted paper size, choose Select (or double-click the desired paper size). You'll return to the document window.

- To *create* a new paper size, choose Create.

- To *edit* the highlighted paper size, choose Edit.

- To *delete* the highlighted paper size, choose Delete, then choose Yes. Skip to step 7.

6. Define or change the paper size (see Options, below). When you're done, choose OK.

7. To select another option, return to step 4. To return to the document window, choose <u>C</u>lose.

OPTIONS   These options are available in the Create Paper Size and Edit Paper Size dialog box for both Windows and WordPerfect printer drivers.

Paper Name   The name you want to appear in the <u>P</u>aper Definitions list.

Type   Choose a paper type from the list of paper types.

Size   Choose a predefined paper size from the <u>S</u>ize dropdown list, or choose User Defined Size and enter a custom size. The default paper size is Letter (8½× 11 inches).

Location   Varies according to printer, but usually includes Manual Feed and Default.

Orientation   Select or deselect Rotated <u>F</u>ont and <u>W</u>ide Form as needed. The sample page in the dialog box provides a graphical view of your selection.

Text Adjustments   If your printer isn't positioning a document correctly, you can adjust the position vertically (T<u>o</u>p) or horizontally (Si<u>d</u>e). Enter the distance you want to adjust the text in each direction. This option may require some trial-and-error.

NOTES   When you select a paper size, WordPerfect inserts a [Paper Sz/Typ:] code at the cursor position.

Definitions are printer-specific. Once you create a definition for a specific printer, you don't have to redefine it.

You can insert more than one paper size code in your document.

Place Paper Size definitions in the document Initial Codes Style of a form file (see the Merge Operations entry).

SEE ALSO   *Binding, Envelope, Initial Codes Style, Labels, Merge Operations, Print, Template*

PARAGRAPH

In WordPerfect, a paragraph is any text that ends with a hard return [HRt]. You can use several features to format the appearance of your paragraphs.

To Format Paragraphs

1. Position the cursor where formatting should start, or select the paragraphs.

2. Choose Layout ➤ Paragraph ➤ Format.

3. Specify the settings you want:

   - To change the first line indent, choose First Line Indent and enter a measurement.

   - To change spacing between paragraphs, choose Spacing Between Paragraphs and enter the number of lines you want between paragraphs.

   - To adjust the paragraph margins relative to the page margins, choose Left Margin Adjustment or Right Margin Adjustment and enter a measurement.

   - To restore all the default settings, choose Clear All.

4. Choose OK.

To use the ruler bar to specify first line indent or paragraph margins, follow these steps:

1. Display the ruler (View ➤ Ruler Bar or Alt+Shift+F3).

2. Position the cursor where formatting should start, or select the paragraphs.

3. Drag markers at the top of the ruler as follows (the status bar will display the name and position of the marker being moved):

- To change the first line indent, drag the indent markers (top left triangle) to a new position.

- To change the left or right paragraph margin, drag the appropriate paragraph adjustment marker (bottom left or right triangle) to a new position.

To Add Paragraph Borders and Fill

1. Position the cursor where formatting should start, or select the paragraphs.

2. Choose Layout ➤ Paragraph ➤ Border/Fill.

3. Choose a border or fill option as described below:

- To change the border style, click the Border Style button or drop-down list and click the style you want. Or, select a border style other than No Border and choose Customize Style to set up a custom border.

- To change the fill style, click the Fill Style button and click the style you want. You can also choose colors from the Foreground and Background buttons.

- To turn the border and fill off, click the Off button.

4. To apply the changes to the current paragraph only, select (check) Apply Border To Current Paragraph Only. To apply the changes to all paragraphs below the cursor position (assuming you didn't select text in step 1), deselect (clear) this option.

5. If necessary, choose OK to return to your document.

NOTES Use Indent features to indent individual paragraphs (see the Indent entry).

SEE ALSO *Indent, Margins, Ruler*

PASSWORD

You can add passwords to your documents to protect them from unauthorized use. A password-protected document cannot be opened or printed from WordPerfect unless the correct password is entered.

To Create or Change a Password

1. Open (File ➤ Open or Ctrl+O) or create (File ➤ New or Ctrl+N) the document.

2. Choose File ➤ Save (Ctrl+S) for new documents or File ➤ Save As (F3) for new or previously saved documents.

3. If you haven't specified a file name for the document, type one into the Filename text box.

4. Select (check) Password Protect and choose OK.

5. Type the password and choose OK. The characters of the password will appear as asterisks when you type them.

6. Retype the password to confirm your entry and choose OK.

7. To activate the protection, close the file (File ➤ Close or Ctrl+F4).

To Remove a Password

1. Open the document (File ➤ Open or Ctrl+O).

2. When prompted, type the password and choose OK.

3.   Choose <u>F</u>ile ➤ Save <u>A</u>s (F3).

4.   Deselect (clear) the <u>P</u>assword Protect check box to remove the X.

5.   Choose OK.

6.   When asked if you want to replace the file, choose <u>Y</u>es.

7.   Close the file (<u>F</u>ile ➤ <u>C</u>lose).

 NOTES   Passwords don't protect the file from being deleted, copied, moved, or renamed, nor do they provide high-level security or encryption.

To change a password, open the file, choose <u>F</u>ile ➤ Save <u>A</u>s, and continue with step 3 of the "To Create or Change a Password" procedure.

SEE ALSO   *File Management, Save/Save As*

PATH AND FILE NAME

Use this feature to insert the current file name or path and file name anywhere in a document. This information is especially useful in page headers and footers.

The file information displayed will instantly reflect the new file or file and path if you copy, move, save, or rename the file.

To Insert the File Name or Path and File Name

1.   If you want to show the file information in a new file, save the file (<u>F</u>ile ➤ <u>S</u>ave).

2.   Position the cursor where you want the information to appear.

3.   Choose <u>I</u>nsert ➤ <u>O</u>ther.

4. To insert the current file name, choose Filename. To insert the full path name of the file, choose Path And Filename.

WordPerfect inserts a [Filename] code at the cursor location.

NOTES See the Save/Save As entry for a discussion on file naming rules.

SEE ALSO *Date/Time; File Management; Headers, Footers, and Watermarks; Save/Save As*

POWER BAR

The power bar (shown below) provides shortcut buttons for many WordPerfect operations.

To Display or Hide the Power Bar

• Choose View ➤ Power Bar.

This toggle option displays the power bar (if it was hidden) or hides it (if it was visible). You can also hide the power bar by right-clicking it and choosing Hide Power Bar.

To Find Out What a Button Does

Move the mouse pointer to the button and look at the title bar at the top of the screen.

To Use the Power Bar

- To choose a power bar button, click it. Or, click the button and drag to highlight the selection you want.

- You can go directly to the dialog boxes for many features by double-clicking their power bar buttons.

- To customize the power bar (add, delete, and move buttons), right-click the power bar and choose Preferences. Or choose File ➤ Preferences and double-click Power Bar. See the Preferences entry for more information.

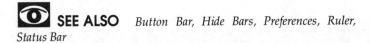 **SEE ALSO**   *Button Bar, Hide Bars, Preferences, Ruler, Status Bar*

PREFERENCES

When you install WordPerfect, many aspects of appearance and behavior are predefined. You can use the Preferences options to change these settings as desired.

To Change Default Preferences

1. Choose File ➤ Preferences.

2. Double-click the icon for the preference you want to change, highlight the icon and press ↵, or choose an option from the Preferences menu in the dialog box. (See Options, below.)

3. Complete the dialog box for the selected preference.

4. Choose OK or Close as necessary to return to the Preferences dialog box.

5. Choose Close to return to your document.

To Go Directly
to a Specific Preferences Dialog Box

1. Point to the button bar, power bar, scroll bar, menu bar, ruler bar, status bar, or Reveal Codes.

2. Right-click the mouse and choose Preferences.

You can also click on buttons in the Preferences button bar to go directly to a preferences dialog box. To display this button bar, do the following:

1. If no button bar is visible, click the View Button Bar button on the power bar, or choose View ➤ Button Bar.

2. Move the mouse to the button bar and right-click.

3. Choose Preferences from the QuickMenu that appears.

OPTIONS The following Preferences options are available:

Display Controls these features of the document window: Document (what to show on the document window, what units of measurement to use, and whether dialog boxes look 3-D); Show ¶ (which "invisible" symbols appear on-screen and whether they initially appear in documents); View/Zoom (default view and zoom size); Reveal Codes (Reveal Codes font, size, color, window size, and other appearance options, and whether Reveal Codes initially appears in documents); Ruler bar (behavior and appearance of the ruler and whether it initially appears in other documents); Merge (appearance of merge codes).

Environment   Controls a variety of items, including user information for comments and document summaries, formatting prompts, deletion confirmations, and warning beeps.

File   Controls default directory locations, file extensions, file names, and whether the QuickList is updated with changes. You can set file preferences for Documents/Backup, Templates, Spreadsheets, Databases, Printers/Labels, Hyphenation, Graphics, and Macros.

Summary   Controls default subject text and descriptive type on document summaries, whether to display descriptive file names in file management dialog boxes, and whether to create a document summary upon saving or exiting.

Button Bar   Lets you Select, Create, Edit, Copy, and Delete button bars and customize the button bar appearance and position. Each button can execute a program feature, play a keyboard script, launch a program or play a macro.

Power Bar   Lets you edit the power bar, select which buttons appear on it, reset it to the default buttons, and customize its appearance.

Status Bar   Lets you edit the status bar, select what information it shows, reset it to the default information, and customize its appearance.

Keyboard   Lets you Select, Create, Edit, Copy, and Delete keyboards. The selected keyboard controls how each key behaves. A key can do nothing, display a text character, execute a program feature, play a keyboard script, launch a program or play a macro.

Menu Bar   Lets you Select, Create, Edit, Copy, and Delete menus. Each menu item can execute a program feature, play a keyboard script, lanch a program, or play a macro.

Writing Tools   Controls which writing tools (Grammatik, Speller, and Thesaurus) appear in the Tools menu.

Print   Controls default print preferences for relative size of fonts (size attribute ratio), number of copies printed and how copies are generated, print quality, print color, the color printing palette used, and whether graphics are printed.

Import   Controls default import settings, including delimiters for fields and records, characters used to enclose text strings, characters to strip during import, code pages, the conversion preferences for some other file formats, and Windows Metafile conversion options.

You can use the Help button in each preferences dialog box to learn more about each preference setting.

 SEE ALSO   *Entries for features mentioned above.*

PRINT

Use the Print command box to print any portion of any document.

To Print the Currently Displayed Document

- Press Ctrl+P, choose File ➤ Print ➤ Print, click on the Print button on the power bar, or press F5 and press P.

To Print Any Portion of Any Document

1. If you want to print a portion of the current document , select that portion.

2. Choose File ➤ Print to get to the Print dialog box.

3. If text is selected, the current printer's Select button is grayed.

4. Under Print Selection, choose what you want to print, (Full Document, Current Page, Multiple Pages, Selected Text, Document Summary, Document On Disk, and so forth).

5.   Optionally, choose the number of copies you want to print and how to generate the copies. For Generated By, you can choose WordPerfect (printed pages will be collated, but printing can be slow) or Printer (generally faster, but printed pages aren't collated).

6.   Under Document Settings, choose a Print Quality (the lower the quality, the faster the print) and Print Color (if you're using a color printer). If you want to print only the text of your document, select Do Not Print Graphics.

7.   You can also choose Options from the Print dialog box, then select from the following options and choose OK to return to the Print dialog box.

Print Document Summary: Prints the document summary, if the current document has one.

Booklet Printing: Prints the document as a booklet or pamphlet, if you've subdivided each page into two columns (see the Subdivide Page entry).

Print In Reverse Order: Prints from last page to first (handy if your printer normally stacks printed pages in reverse order).

Print Odd/Even Pages: Useful for printing pages back-to-back on a non-duplex printer. That is, you can print the odd-numbered pages first, then put those pages back in the printer and print only the even-numbered pages.

Output Bin Options: If your printer has a deluxe output bin, you can activate that bin's Sort, Group, and Jogger capabilities. If you have multiple bins, you can select a bin as well.

8.   Choose Print when you've made all of your selections and are ready to print.

9. If you opted to print Multiple Pages, you'll be prompted for a range of pages. You can enter specific pages separated by a comma or indicate a range of pages with a hyphen. For example, **3,5,20-30** would print page 3, then page 5, then pages 20 through 30. Choose Print again to start printing.

10. If you selected Document On Disk, type (or select) the name of the document you want to print in the Filename text box. Enter any specific pages you want printed or accept the default (all pages), then choose Print again to start printing.

To Send a Fax from WordPerfect

You must have a Fax board installed according to the manufacturer's instructions. Then, to fax a WordPerfect document directly from disk or from your screen, follow the steps above, but choose your Fax board driver as the printer to use in step 3. Complete the rest of the steps normally, and respond to any prompts that your Fax driver displays on the screen.

 SEE ALSO   *Booklets and Pamphlets, Preferences*

QUICKFINDER

QuickFinder can search rapidly through files and QuickFinder indexes for certain words, phrases, or patterns. The result will be a list of files that contain the information you searched for.

For fastest searching, create and use QuickFinder indexes.

To Open the QuickFinder

You can get to the QuickFinder using any method below:

- Choose File ➤ QuickFinder to open the QuickFinder dialog box. The sections below describe this method.

- Go to any Open File, Select File, or Save As dialog box (for example, choose File ➤ Open). Click the QuickFinder button.

- Start from the Program Manager and double-click the QuickFinder File Indexer icon in the WPWin 6.0 group window.

To Create a QuickFinder Index

1. Choose File ➤ QuickFinder.

2. Choose Indexer ➤ Create.

3. Type an index name and choose OK.

4. To add a file or files to the index, type the file, directory name, or wildcard pattern into the Add Directory Or File text box. (Alternatively, you can choose Browse, then highlight the file or directory you want.)

5. To include subtrees of a selected directory, select (check) Include Subtree.

6. Choose Add. (If you add a file or directory accidentally, highlight it in the Directories To Index list and choose Remove.)

7. Repeat steps 4–6 as needed.

8. To choose the amount of detail in the index, choose Options, select the options you want, and choose OK.

9. To generate the index, choose Generate. After the index is complete, choose OK, then choose Close twice.

To Manage QuickFinder Indexes

1. Choose File ➤ QuickFinder.

2. Choose Indexer.

3. Highlight an index name in the Index Names list.

4. Take one of the actions below:

- To regenerate the highlighted index, choose Generate. Either select update Index With New Or Modified Files or select Index All Files. Choose OK.

- To edit the highlighted index, choose Edit. Proceed as for creating an index above (start with step 4).

- To get information about the index, to delete, rename, or move the index, or to change the index preferences, choose the Options button and select the option you want.

5. Repeat steps 3 and 4 as needed.

6. Choose Close in the QuickFinder File Indexer dialog box, and Close again in the QuickFinder dialog box.

To Search with QuickFinder

1. Choose File ➤ QuickFinder.

2. In the File Pattern text box, specify a file pattern.

3. In the Search For text box, type the word, phrase, or pattern you want to search for. You can use the button at the end of the text box to specify Operators, Document Components, Case Sensitivity, and Closeness of Words. You can leave this text box blank to search for any files that match the other criteria specified in the QuickFinder dialog box, regardless of the text in those files.

4. Use the Search In pop-up list button to specify where QuickFinder should search (Directory, Disk, Subtree, or QuickFinder Index). If you choose Disk or QuickFinder Index, select the drive or the name of the index in the drop-down list box.

5. To limit the search to WordPerfect documents only, select (check) WordPerfect Documents only.

6. To limit the search to files that were created or changes in a specific date range, enter the range in the From and To text boxes.

7. Choose Find.

8. If QuickFinder finds a match, the Search Results List dialog box will open. You can then do any of the following:

   - To view files without opening them, choose View and click on or highlight files in the Search Results list.

   - To return to the QuickFinder dialog box, choose Quick-Finder.

   - To change the sort order of files, choose Sort Setup.

   - To do file management tasks, choose File Options. (See the File Management entry.)

   - To save the search results, select (check) Save Search Results.

   - To rearrange the Search Results list, drag the heading buttons. You can use the buttons to move, resize, and delete columns. Click the < and > buttons to scroll columns to the left or right.

OPTIONS   The Options button in the QuickFinder dialog box provides these capabilities:

Summary Fields   Shows or hides document summary fields. When document summary fields appear, you can include them in your search.

Last Search Results   Returns to the most recent list of saved Search Results.

Clear   Clears the Search For text box.

Load Search Query Lets you load a saved search query.

Save Search Query Lets you save a search query.

Delete Search Query Lets you delete a saved search query.

 NOTES If you change the contents of indexed files or directories, you should regenerate the appropriate QuickFinder indexes before using them again. The KickOff program offers a handy method for updating QuickFinder indexes on a regular basis (see the KickOff entry).

SEE ALSO *File Management, Find, KickOff, Open, Save/ Save As*

QUICK FORMAT

Quick Format lets you quickly format other text in your document with the same fonts and Paragraph styles that are in effect at the cursor position.

To Quick-Format Text

1. Place the cursor in text that has the font or Paragraph style you want to copy.

2. Choose Layout ➤ QuickFormat, right-click and choose QuickFormat, or click the QuickFormat button in the WordPerfect button bar.

3. Choose one of the options below:

- To copy only the fonts and print attributes to other text, choose Fonts And Attributes.

- To copy only the Paragraph styles to other text, choose Paragraph Styles. Paragraph styles are created and applied via the Styles command (Layout ➤ Styles).

172 QuickList

- To copy the fonts, attributes, and Paragraph styles to other text, choose <u>B</u>oth.

4. Choose OK.

5. Use your mouse to select the text you want to quick-format. When you release the mouse button, WordPerfect will copy the formatting codes from the original text to the selected text. Repeat this step until you've selected and reformatted as much text as you want.

6. To turn off QuickFormat, repeat step 2.

 NOTES WordPerfect quick-formats by *copying* codes and/or <u>P</u>aragraph styles from the original text into the selected text. If you later change the format of the original paragraph, WordPerfect will adjust the other text that you quick formatted *only* if you chose the <u>P</u>aragraph Styles or <u>B</u>oth option in step 3.

SEE ALSO *Font, Paragraph, Styles, Template*

QUICKLIST

The QuickList lets you assign descriptive, easy-to-remember names for frequently-used directory and file names. You can select a QuickList entry instead of typing file and directory names into dialog boxes.

Many QuickList entries are created automatically when you define directory and file locations in the File Preferences dialog box.

To Use the QuickList

1. Go to the Open File, Select File, or Save As dialog box (e.g., choose <u>F</u>ile ➤ <u>O</u>pen).

2.   If the QuickList isn't visible in the dialog box, choose QuickList ➤ Show Both (or QuickList ➤ Show QuickList).

3.   To select an entry in the QuickList, click it. Or choose QuickList and highlight the entry you want. This fills in the Filename or Directory Name text box with the file, directory, or wildcard name assigned to the QuickList entry.

4.   Complete the dialog box as required by whatever operation you chose in step 1.

To Add, Change, and Delete QuickList Entries

1.   Go to the Open File, Select File, or Save As dialog box (e.g., choose File ➤ Open). If necessary, select QuickList ➤ Show QuickList or QuickList ➤ Show Both, so that you can see the QuickList. Show Both is usually the best choice.

2.   Take any of the actions below:

- To create a new entry, choose QuickList ➤ Add Item. In the Directory/Filename text box, type a directory name, file name, or wildcard pattern; or use the file button on the dialog box to locate and fill in a directory name. In the Description text box, enter a description for the entry (or accept the description that appears automatically). Choose OK.

- To edit an existing entry, highlight the entry and choose QuickList ➤ Add Item. Proceed as for creating a new entry.

- To delete an entry, highlight the entry and choose QuickList ➤ Add Item

3.   Repeat step 3 as needed. When you're done, choose OK to return to the Open/Save As Setup dialog box, then continue your current operation.

4.   Choose Cancel to close the Open File, Select File, or Save As dialog box.

SEE ALSO   *File Management, Open, Preferences, Save/ Save As*

QUICKMENU

WordPerfect displays a QuickMenu when you right-click a certain area of the screen (see Notes, below). Options on the QuickMenu are relevant to the area of the WordPerfect screen you click.

To Use a QuickMenu

1. Point to a "hot spot" area (see Notes, below) on the document window or a file management dialog box and right-click the mouse.

2. To choose an option from the menu, click on it with the left or right mouse button or type the option's underlined letter.

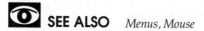 **NOTES**   The following hot spot areas offer QuickMenus: normal document text, far left edge of document window, Reveal Codes, scroll bars, status bar, button bar, power bar, menu bar, ruler bar, tables, graphics boxes and lines, comments, and list in the file management dialog boxes.

 SEE ALSO   *Menus, Mouse*

REPEAT

The Repeat feature lets you repeat a keystroke, command, or macro a specified number of times. Not all actions can be repeated.

To Repeat an Action

1. Move the cursor to the location where an action will be repeated.

2. Choose Edit ➤ Repeat.

3. Optionally, specify the number of times to repeat the action.

4. If you want the number to be the new default setting, choose Use As Default.

5. Choose OK.

6. Press a key, choose a menu option, click a button on the button bar, or run a macro.

 SEE ALSO   *Button Bar, Macros, Menus*

REPLACE

Use Replace to locate any sequence of characters or codes and change it to something else.

To Replace Text or Codes

1. To be safe, save the document (File ➤ Save).

2. Move the cursor to where replacement should start or select only the text to be affected.

3. Choose Edit ➤ Replace (Ctrl+F2).

4. To change a *specific code* (such as Times New Roman Italic) to a different code (such as Univers (W1)) or to delete it altogether, choose <u>T</u>ype ➤ <u>S</u>pecific Codes. Select the code you want to search for, then select the code you want to replace it with. (You can delete certain specific codes by checking the Replace with <u>N</u>othing box.) Skip to step 7.

5. To change general codes and/or specific text, position the cursor in the F<u>i</u>nd text box and take any action below:

- To search for a *word or phrase,* type that word or phrase. (Press Ctrl+W if you want to insert a WordPerfect character.)

- To match *whole words only,* choose <u>M</u>atch ➤ <u>W</u>hole Word.

- To match exact *upper- and lowercase* letters in the search string, choose <u>M</u>atch ➤ <u>C</u>ase.

- To insert a *general code* (such as [HRt]) or a *wildcard pattern,* choose <u>M</u>atch ➤ C<u>o</u>des, and highlight the code you want. (Wildcard codes are * *(Many Char)* and ? *(One Char)*). Choose <u>I</u>nsert.

6. In the Replace <u>W</u>ith text box, specify the replacement text. You can type text and WordPerfect characters (Ctrl+W), and choose Replace options (<u>C</u>ase, <u>F</u>ont, and C<u>o</u>des). If you want to *delete* the search string, leave the Replace <u>W</u>ith text box blank.

7. Optionally, choose the search direction (either <u>D</u>irection ➤ <u>F</u>orward or <u>D</u>irection ➤ <u>B</u>ackward).

8. Optionally, choose where the search will start, how much text is searched, or how many changes are made by selecting items from the <u>O</u>ptions menu.

9. Start the replacement as described below:

- To find and highlight the next (or previous) match, *without* making any changes, choose <u>F</u>ind.

- To replace one match of the search string, then highlight the next (or previous) match, choose <u>R</u>eplace.

- To replace all matches at once (up to the limit specified by <u>O</u>ptions ➤ Limit <u>N</u>umber Of Changes), choose Replace <u>A</u>ll.

- To close the dialog box without making more changes, choose <u>C</u>lose.

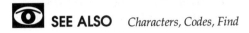 **SEE ALSO** *Characters, Codes, Find*

REVEAL CODES

WordPerfect uses codes to implement most formatting features. These codes are hidden unless you open the Reveal Codes window, which appears in the lower part of your screen.

To Turn Reveal Codes On and Off

Use one of the following methods:

- Choose <u>V</u>iew ➤ Reveal <u>C</u>odes (Alt+F3).

- Or, if Reveal Codes is on, right-click the Reveal Codes window and choose <u>H</u>ide Reveal Codes.

To Use the Reveal Codes Window

You can take any of these actions when the Reveal Codes window is visible:

- To *edit text*, position the cursor in the document window or the Reveal Codes window and edit normally.

- To see a brief *description of a code*, point to it with your mouse and look at the title bar at the top of the screen.

- To *delete a code*, click on it or move the cursor just to the right of the code. Press Backspace (if the cursor is just to the left of the code, press Delete instead), or drag the code above the Reveal Codes window and release the mouse button. Deleting one paired code deletes both codes.

- To go directly to a *dialog box* for editing the code, double-click the code. (This works for many codes.)

- To *move a single code,* delete the code. Position the cursor where you want the code to reappear and choose Edit ➤ Undelete (Ctrl+Shift+Z).

- To *copy or move one or more single codes,* select the code(s) and choose Edit ➤ Copy (Ctrl+C) or Edit ➤ Cut (Ctrl+X). Position the cursor where you want the code(s) to reappear and choose Edit ➤ Paste (Ctrl+V). You can only move or copy single codes, not paired codes.

- To customize the Reveal Codes window, right-click the Reveal Codes window and choose Preferences.

- To resize the Reveal Codes window, move the mouse pointer to the dividing line between the normal document window and the Reveal Codes window (the pointer changes to a two-headed vertical arrow). Now drag the divider up or down and release the mouse button.

NOTES   The example below shows a screen with the Reveal Codes window open. The top section is the normal document window. The lower portion, which displays codes and text, is the Reveal Codes window.

The Reveal Codes cursor is a rectangle that appears just to the left or right of characters and codes as you move through the document window. The cursors on both screens are at exactly the same place in the document, and both move together. Codes usually appear as buttons to distinguish them from text.

You can use Reveal Codes to check for proper formatting, delete a code, or make sure relevant codes are included when you select text (see the Selecting Text entry).

👁 **SEE ALSO** *Codes, Delete, Document Window, Preferences, Selecting Text, Undelete, Windows*

RULER

The ruler (shown in Figure 5) provides shortcuts for formatting paragraphs, margins, tab stops, columns, and tables. You can also right-click or double-click the ruler or its markers to reach relevant dialog boxes.

The ruler has two sections: the paragraph, margins, tables, and columns area on top, and the tab stops on the bottom. (Figure 5 does not show the tables and columns markers. These appear at the top of the ruler.)

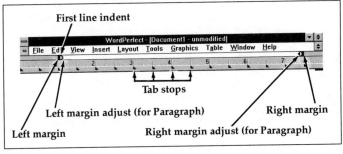

Figure 5: The Ruler

To Turn the Ruler On and Off

- Choose <u>V</u>iew ➤ <u>R</u>uler Bar (Alt+Shift+F3).
- Or, right-click the ruler and choose <u>H</u>ide Ruler Bar.

To Use the Ruler

General procedures for using the ruler are listed below. See the specific entries listed in the See Also section below for details.

1.   Move the cursor to where you want to change the settings, or select text to limit your changes to a block.

2.   Take one of the actions below:

   - To set a new tab stop, right-click the mouse in the tab stops area, select a tab type, then click the mouse at the correct spot on the bottom of the ruler. A new tab stop marker will appear.

   - To delete a tab stop, drag its marker down off the ruler.

   - To move a tab stop, margin, paragraph margin, or first-line indent, or to resize a column, drag the appropriate marker to its new position. The status bar at the bottom of the screen will indicate what you are changing and its current position. Release the mouse button when the marker is positioned properly.

NOTES   To customize the ruler, right-click it and choose <u>P</u>references.

SEE ALSO   *Codes, Columns, Margins, Paragraph, Preferences, Tables, Tabs*

SAVE/SAVE AS

Documents are held in the computer's memory only until you save them. To prevent loss of work, you must save your changes before you close a document window, exit WordPerfect, or turn off your computer.

To Save a Document

1. Choose File ➤ Save (Ctrl+S) or File ➤ Save As (F3), or click the Save button in the power bar.

2. If you chose File ➤ Save for a file that was previously saved, WordPerfect will save the file under the previous name and won't prompt further. If the file is new or you chose File ➤ Save As, continue with the remaining steps.

3. In the Filename text box, enter the file name or full path name for the document. You can also use any technique discussed in the File Management entry to help you fill in the text box.

4. If you want to save the file in a non-WordPerfect format (e.g., WordStar or ASCII text), choose the format from the Format drop-down list.

5. Choose OK.

6. If the file name already exists on disk, WordPerfect will ask if you want to replace the existing file. Choose Yes to replace it or No to return to step 3.

NOTES   File names can have up to eight characters, plus a period and a one- to three-letter extension. Full path names include a drive letter, the name of each directory above the file, separated by backslashes (\), and the file name.

Never use spaces in path names, file names, or extensions. Avoid using extensions with special meanings to DOS, Windows, or WordPerfect (such as .COM or .EXE).

Unless you enter a full path name, the file is saved in your default directory. If you omit the extension, WordPerfect uses the default extension defined in File Preferences.

Sample file names are   MEMO   MEMO.WPD   MYSTUFF.1

Sample path names are   D:\MEMOS\MYSTUFF.1   A:MEMO.WPD

You can use Save As to add, change, or remove passwords from a file (see the Password entry).

When you close a document window (File ➤ Close or Ctrl+F4) or exit WordPerfect (File ➤ Exit or Alt+F4), WordPerfect will prompt you to save changes if you haven't done so yet. Choose Yes to save the changes, No to discard changes, or Cancel to return to the document.

See the Master Document entry to learn about saving master documents and subdocuments.

👁 **SEE ALSO**   *Combine Documents, Document Summary, Exit, File Management, Master Document, Password, Path and Filename, Preferences*

SELECTING TEXT

Selecting text lets you identify text to be moved, copied, or deleted, and also lets you activate print attributes (bold, italic), styles, and other features *after* you've typed the text. Selected text appears highlighted on screen.

To Select Text with the Mouse

1. Position the I-beam at one end of the text you wish to block.

2. Hold down the left mouse button and drag the mouse pointer to the other end of the text. The text will be highlighted.

3. Release the left mouse button.

See the Mouse entry for other selection methods.

To Select Text with the Keyboard

1. Optionally, turn on Reveal Codes (Alt+F3) so you can be sure appropriate codes are included or excluded from the selection.

2. Position the cursor at one end of the text.

3. Use any of these techniques to select the text:

- Hold down Shift and use the arrow, Home, End or other cursor-positioning keys to extend the selection.
- Choose options from the Edit ➤ Select menus.
- Press F8 and use cursor-positioning keys to extend the selection.
- Press F2 (Find), choose Action ➤ Extend Selection, type the text or codes to extend the selection to, and choose Find Next.

NOTES After selecting text, you can choose almost any formatting option that WordPerfect offers. Options that aren't available for selected text will be dimmed in the menus.

If you type a character while a block is selected, the entire block will be replaced with that character.

To "unselect" selected text without performing an operation, move the cursor, click the left mouse button, or press F8.

 SEE ALSO   *Cursor, Mouse*

SHORTCUT KEYS

Use keystroke combinations from the keyboard to accomplish common tasks quickly. You can customize the keyboard layout to create shortcut keys (see the Preferences entry).

NOTES   Shortcut keys are listed on the menus to the right of the command names.

To see a complete list of shortcut keys assigned to a keyboard that you've created, choose File ➤ Preferences and double-click Keyboard. Highlight the keyboard you want to look at and choose Edit.

 SEE ALSO   *Menus, Preferences*

SORTING AND SELECTING

Use Sort to arrange information into a more meaningful order or to extract or isolate specific information from documents. You can sort lines, paragraphs, table rows, parallel columns, and merge data file records.

To Sort and Extract

1.   If you'll be selecting records, make a copy of the file first (File ➤ Save As).

2. Position the cursor anywhere in the document text (to sort the entire document or a file on disk) or inside a table or columns (to sort the table or columns). Or select the text or rows you want to sort.

3. Choose Tools ➤ Sort (Alt+F9).

4. Specify the Input File (current document or a file on disk). (After specifying a file on disk, you can use the View Input File button to view it.)

5. Specify the Output File (current document or a file on disk). When specifying a document on disk, be careful not to use the original file or any other file you care about.

6. Choose a type of record in the Sort By area of the dialog box, or accept the suggested record type (the suggested record type is usually correct. See below for details).

7. Define each sort key, including the key number, type, sort order, and other information. (See "To Define a Sort Key," below.)

8. To sort uppercase letters before lowercase letters, select (check) Uppercase First.

9. If you want to extract records, enter the record selection criteria in the Select Records text box. (See "To Select Records," below.) To extract records without sorting them first, select (check) Select Without Sorting.

10. Choose OK to start the sort.

If your sort didn't work out as expected, press Ctrl+Z immediately to undo the changes. (This works only when you're sorting output to the current document.)

To Define a Sort Key

Use sort keys to specify which piece of the record to sort by. You can have up to nine sort keys (Key1, Key2, Key3, …, Key9). Key1 has first priority, Key2 second priority, and so on.

1. To add, insert, delete, or select a key, go to the Sort dialog box and use any of the techniques below:

   - To add a new key to the bottom of the list, choose the Add key button.

   - To insert a key, click where the new key should appear and choose Insert Key.

   - To delete a key, click the key to be deleted and choose Delete Key.

   - To select the key you want to change, use the Add Key or Insert Key button (as described just above), click anywhere on the key, or press Alt plus the key number (e.g., Alt+1). The selected key number will be marked with a > character.

2. Specify the key *Type:* either Alpha (numbers and letters) or Numeric (numbers, dollar signs, commas, and periods only).

3. Specify the *Sort Order:* either Ascending (A–Z, 0–9, negative to positive) or Descending (Z–A, 9–0, positive to negative).

4. Specify which column, cell, field, line, and word to sort by in each key (as appropriate). These items are numbered from left to right within the record. To number from right to left, use a negative number. For example, Word -1 is the last word, Word -2 is the second-to-last word, and so on.

To Select Records

Use the Select Records text box to define selection criteria that will select (isolate) specific records. *Warning: Records that don't meet the the Select Records criteria will be deleted if you extract them to the current file, or if you overwrite the input file with the extracted version of the file!*

Each selection criterion has these components:

- A *key* specified as "key*n*" where *n* is a number (e.g., *key1*). Use *"keyg"* instead of a key number for a global selection where any field can qualify (e.g., keyg=Bermuda will match "Bermuda" in any field).

- A *selection operator*. The operators are | (OR), & (AND), =
  (equal), <> (not equal), > (greater than), < (less than), >=
  (greater than or equal), and <= (less than or equal).

- A *value* to match. Values can be numbers and/or letters.

You can combine key statements, such as *Key1>=Jones & Key1<=Smith*.
Selection is done from left to right unless you use parentheses for
grouping, as in *key5=male & (key1=Smith | key1=Jones)*.

Sample selection criteria are shown in Table V.

Table V: Sample Selection Criteria

CRITERIA	MEANING
key1=Smith	key3=Arizona	Selects all Smiths and all Arizona records.
key1=Smith&key3=Arizona	Selects all Smiths in Arizona.
key3=Arizona	Selects all Arizona records.
key3<>Arizona	Selects all residents that don't live in Arizona.
key3>M	Selects residents in states that start with M or later in the alphabet (e.g., Maryland, Michigan, Nebraska, and Washington, but not Arizona, California, or Georgia)
key3<M	Selects residents in states with names that are earlier than M in the alphabet (e.g., Arizona, California, and Georgia, but not Maryland, Michigan, Nebraska, or Washington.
key4<=92123	Selects residents with zip codes less than or equal to 92123 in key4.

Table V: Sample Selection Criteria (continued)

CRITERIA	MEANING
key4>=92123	Selects residents with zip codes greater than or equal to 92123 in key4.
key3=Utah & key1=Smith | key1=Brown	Selects Smiths in Utah and all Browns.
key3=Utah & (key1=Smith | key1=Brown)	Selects Smiths and Browns in Utah.

NOTES *Records* are the lines, paragraphs, rows in parallel columns or tables, or text blocks to be sorted. Each record can be further broken down into cells, columns, fields, lines, and/or words.

Fields are separated by tabs or indents in lines and paragraphs, and by ENDFIELD codes in merge records. In tables, each cell is a field. Records can contain many fields. Each corresponding field should contain the same type of information.

There are five different kinds of records:

Line Each line is a record that ends with a hard return [HRt]. Records are divided into fields and words.

Paragraph Each paragraph is a record. Paragraphs must end with at least two hard returns [HRt]. Records are divided into lines, fields, and words.

Merge Record (non-tabular merge file) Records are separated by ENDRECORD codes. Records are divided into fields, lines, and words.

Column (parallel columns) Each record is a row of columns. Records are divided into columns, lines, and words.

Table Row Each row is a record. Records are divided into cells, lines, and words.

Lines are separated by hard or soft returns.

Words are separated by spaces, forward slashes (/), or hard hyphens (Ctrl+—) within a line or field. To select multiple words for sorting as if they were single words, place a hard space (Ctrl+spacebar) between the words. This is useful when sorting names like "Edward Merriweather III" and "John Jones" by last name.

Columns are separated by hard column breaks [HCol] entered by pressing Ctrl+↵.

Codes within a record will be sorted along with the record. This may affect the appearance of text between paired codes.

To sort text according to a certain language, insert a Language code before the text you're sorting (see the Language entry).

To sort dates, treat the month, day, and year as separate words and divide dates with forward slashes (07/08/94) or hard hyphens (07-08-94). To enter a hard hyphen, press Ctrl+-.

SEE ALSO   *Columns, Hyphenation, Language, Merge Operations, Spaces (Hard and Soft), Tables*

If your computer has sound capabilities, you can add sounds to your WordPerfect documents. Two methods are available: Object Linking and Embedding (see the Object Linking and Embedding entry) and WordPerfect's Insert ➤ Sound feature.

To Add a Sound Clip

1. Move the cursor to where you want to put the sound clip.

2. Choose Insert ➤ Sound ➤ Insert.

3. Optionally, enter a name for the sound clip in the Name text box.

4. In the File text box, type the name of the file that contains the sound clip, or use the file button to locate the sound clip. (Sound clips are often stored in C:\WINDOWS or its subdirectories.)

5. To have the sound change if you change the sound file on disk and to keep your document smaller, select Link To File On Disk. To prevent the sound from changing if you change the sound file on disk, choose Store In Document (your document will be larger).

6. Choose OK. A sound clip comment will appear at the cursor position.

To Play a Sound

Click the sound clip icon, or sound clip comment box, or follow the steps below:

1. Choose Insert ➤ Sound to open the Sound Clips dialog box.

2. Highlight the sound clip you want to play in the Sound Clips In Document list.

3. Click the Play button. You can also use the Rew (Rewind), FF (Fast Forward), and Stop buttons and the Playback Controls scroll bar to listen to the sound again.

4. Choose Close when you're done.

OPTIONS   These options are available in the Sound Clips dialog box:

Record   Opens the Windows Sound Recorder, which lets you record sounds, create special sound effects, and save sounds to disk. See your Windows documentation for information.

Edit Desc. Lets you change the name (description) of a sound clip.

Transcribe Lets you play back sounds while you work in the document window. Use this option to type into your document while listening to the sound (this is like taking dictation). You can also reach this option by right-clicking the sound comment icon and choosing Transcribe from the QuickMenu.

Delete Lets you delete the highlighted sound clip.

Save As Lets you save to disk a sound clip that's stored in the document.

 SEE ALSO   *Hypertext, Macros, Object Linking and Embedding*

SPACES (HARD AND SOFT)

You can insert hard or soft spaces between words. Use hard spaces [HSpace] to have more than one word treated as a single word for formatting, hyphenation, and sorting. Use soft spaces to treat each word separately.

To Insert a Soft or Hard Space

1. Position the cursor where you want to insert the space.

2. For a *soft space*, press the spacebar. For a *hard space*, press Ctrl+spacebar.

 SEE ALSO   *Hyphenation, Sorting and Selecting*

SPELLER

Speller can identify and replace spelling errors, repeated words, words containing numbers, and capitalization errors. You can also have Speller suggest words that fit a particular pattern.

To Start a Spelling Check

1. Optionally, move the cursor to the word or page you want to check, or select a block of text.

2. Choose Tools ➤ Speller (Ctrl+F1), or click the Speller button on the power bar.

3. Optionally, choose Check from the Speller menu bar and select the scope of the spell check (Word, Sentence, Paragraph, Page, Document, To End Of Document, Selected Text, Text Entry Box, Number Of Pages).

4. If you wish, select or deselect items on the Options menu. (See Options, below.)

5. Choose Start to begin the spell check.

6. Respond to prompts that appear (see next section).

To Correct Misspelled Words

During a spell check, Speller will highlight any word that it can't find in the main or supplementary dictionaries. The Suggestions will show possible replacements for the misspelled word. You can then choose from the options below:

- Select the correct word in the Suggestions list and click Replace.

- Click the Add To pop-up list button and choose the dictionary you want to add the word to. Select Add to add the word to the dictionary.

- Select Skip Once to skip this occurrence of the word.

- Select Skip Always to skip all occurrences of the word.

- Edit the word in the Replace With text box and click Replace.

- List other suggestions. Enter a word or word pattern (see Notes, below) in the Replace With text box, then choose Suggest.

- Click in the document window and make changes. Click Resume to resume spell checking.

To Use Different Speller Dictionaries

WordPerfect uses a built-in main dictionary (WPUS.LEX), a supplementary dictionary (usually named WPSPELUS.SUP), and the document supplemental dictionary (stored in the document). The main dictionary usually is stored in C:\WPC20. The WPSPELUS.SUP dictionary usually resides in C:\WINDOWS. You can create supplementary dictionaries of your own and buy additional main dictionaries from WordPerfect Corporation.

To Choose a Different Dictionary

1. Choose Dictionaries from the Speller dialog menu bar.

2. Choose Main or Supplementary.

3. Choose an option below:

   - To *create* a new supplementary dictionary or *insert* an existing dictionary into the Dictionaries In Search Order list, highlight the position where the dictionary name should appear, and choose Add or Create. Respond to additional prompts.

   - To edit a dictionary, highlight the dictionary name in the list and choose Edit. You can then add, edit, or delete keywords that the Speller will skip, replace, or offer alternatives for during a spell check.

- To delete a dictionary from the chain, highlight the dictionary name and choose <u>D</u>elete, then <u>Y</u>es.

- To specify a different language for the chain, choose <u>L</u>anguage, select the language, and choose OK. The language module must already be installed according to the manufacturer's instructions.

4. When you're ready to return to the Speller dialog box, choose <u>C</u>lose.

OPTIONS You can choose these items from the O<u>p</u>tions menu before starting a spell check:

Words With Numbers Enables or disables checking for embedded numbers in words.

Duplicate Words Enables or disables checking for double words.

Irregular Capitalization Enables or disables checking for irregular capitalization.

Exhaustive Enables or disables display of all possible suggestions in languages where limited suggestions are usually displayed.

Auto Replace When deselected, Speller will prompt before changing a word that you've previously designated as "auto-replace." When selected, Speller will auto-replace without prompting first.

Document Dictionary When selected, Speller will not stop at misspelled words that you previously added to the supplementary dictionary that's attached to the current document. When deselected, Speller will stop at misspelled words that you previously added to this dictionary.

Beep on Misspelled Enables or disables a beep sound when the Speller finds a misspelled word.

NOTES You can enter word patterns in the Replace <u>W</u>ith text box, and then choose S<u>u</u>ggest to see a list of words that "sound like" the pattern you entered.

A word pattern is composed of characters and wildcards. Use a question mark (?) to represent a single character and an asterisk (*) to represent multiple characters. For example, *chil?* results in *child, Chile, chili,* and *chill*; while **kmarks* retrieves *bookmarks* and *pockmarks*.

To temporarily disable the writing tools, including Speller, move the cursor to where you want to disable the tools, or select a block of text. Choose Tools ➤ Language, check the Disable Writing Tools… box, and choose OK.

 SEE ALSO   *Grammatik, Hyphenation, Language, Preferences, Thesaurus*

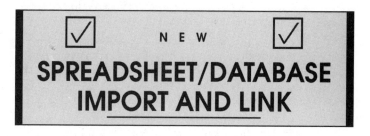

SPREADSHEET/DATABASE IMPORT AND LINK

You can import (copy) or link information from a spreadsheet, database, or ASCII delimited text file into your WordPerfect document. Linked files will be updated in your WordPerfect document automatically whenever they change in the underlying data file. Imported files won't be updated in your document when the underlying files change.

To Import or Link Data

1. Move the cursor to where you want the data to appear in your document.

2. Choose Insert ➤ Spreadsheet/Database.

3. To import the data, choose Import. To link the data, choose Create Link.

4. Use the Data Type pop-up list button to select the type of
data to import or link. You can choose Spreadsheet, any of
several database formats, or ASCII Delimited Text.

5. Use the Import As or Link As pop-up list button to select
the format of the data in the WordPerfect document. Your
options are Table, Text, and (non-tabular) Merge Data File.

6. In the Filename text box, specify the name of the data file
to import or link, or use the file button to locate the file.
Press Tab.

7. Depending on the Data Type, you can further tailor the
imported/linked data:

- For *spreadsheets*, you can select a named range or specify a range.

- For *databases*, you can select (check) the fields you want
and use field names as headings. You can even define a
Query to limit the imported/linked data to specific conditions in up to three fields.

- For *ASCII delimited text*, you can change the field and record delimiters, the characters that surround (encapsu-
late) strings of text, and the characters to strip upon
import.

8. Choose OK to import or link the data.

OPTIONS These options are also available on the Insert ➤
Spreadsheet/Database menu:

Edit Link Lets you edit the link for the data the cursor is in.
After choosing this option, follow steps 4–8 above to edit a link.

Update Lets you update all data links at once.

Options Lets you choose whether to update the links when
you retrieve the document and whether to show the link icons.

NOTES A spreadsheet range is a rectangular section of
a spreadsheet file. To specify a range, enter the cell addresses of the
top-left and bottom-right corners, separated by a colon, period, or
two periods (e.g., A1:F35, A1.F35, or A1..F35). If the spreadsheet file

has named ranges, the names will appear in the list box and you can select the name instead of typing the cell addresses.

To break a link but leave the data in your document, turn on Reveal Codes (Alt+F3) and delete the appropriate [Link] code.

Data that's linked or imported as text will be separated into columns by tabs and into rows by hard returns.

To set the default delimiters and characters for imported ASCII delimited text files, choose File ➤ Preferences and double-click Import.

 SEE ALSO   *Merge Operations, Object Linking and Embedding, Preferences, Tables*

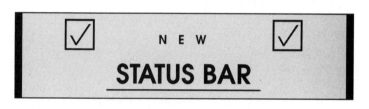

The status bar appears at the bottom of the WordPerfect window to provide information about the current status of your WordPerfect document. Initially the bar shows the current font, general status information such as whether you're in Insert mode or Typeover mode, whether a macro is being recorded, whether text is selected, and the location of the cursor within the document. You can display, hide, and customize the status bar.

To Display or Hide the Status Bar

- Choose View ➤ Status Bar (to display or hide the bar).
- Or, right-click the status bar and choose Hide Status Bar (to hide the bar).

To Customize the Status Bar

- Choose File ➤ Preferences and double-click the Status Bar icon, or right-click the status bar and choose Preferences.

 SEE ALSO *Preferences*

STYLES

Styles let you apply consistent formatting to your text. Any changes that you make to a style will be reflected automatically in any text formatted with that style.

To Create a Style

1. Choose Layout ➤ Styles, press Alt+F8, or click the Styles button in the WordPerfect button bar. The Style List dialog box opens.

2. To choose which styles appear in the Style List and where style changes will be saved, choose Options ➤ Setup, select any options below, then choose OK.

   - *Display Styles From* options control which styles appear in the Style List. Your options are Current Document, Default Template, Supplemental Template, and System Styles. System styles are WordPerfect's built-in styles (you can edit these).

   - *Default Location* options determine where WordPerfect saves your style changes. You can choose Current Document (the default), Default Template, or Supplemental Template.

3. Choose Create.

4. In the Style Name text box, type a name for the style. (Do not assign style names that are already used for other styles in other templates and documents).

5. In the Description text box, type a description of the style.

6. Choose a style type from the Type pop-up list. Your options are Character (Paired), Paragraph (Paired), or Document (Open). (See Options, below.)

7. Optionally, choose options that control what the Enter (↵) key does in a Character or Paragraph style (it's often easiest to skip this step). See "To Control the Enter Key," below.

8. To have the style activate some new format at its end, select (check) Show 'Off Codes'.

9. To define the formatting codes and text, choose Contents. If you checked Show 'Off Codes' in step 8, enter codes that turn the style on before the first [HPg] code, and codes that turn it off after the [HPg] code. See "To Enter Style Codes in the Contents Box," below.

10. When you're done, choose OK to return to the Style List.

11. Choose Close to return to your document.

To Apply a Style

1. Move the cursor to where the style should begin, or select a block of text.

2. Choose Layout ➤ Styles, press Alt+F8, or click the Styles button in the WordPerfect button bar.

3. Highlight the style you want and choose Apply, or double-click the style.

To Enter Style Codes in the Contents Box

Use any technique below to enter formatting text and codes in the Contents box:

- Choose formatting features from the menus or use the usual shortcut keys.

- Type in any text or special characters (Ctrl+W) that you want WordPerfect to insert automatically.

- To delete a code, move the cursor to it and press Delete or drag the code out of the Contents box.

- To see what your style will look like without the hidden codes, deselect Reveal Codes. To redisplay the codes in the Contents box, select Reveal Codes again.

- To insert an existing style into the one you're creating, press Alt+F8, highlight a style from the Style List, and choose Apply.

- To insert a page break [HPg] into the style, press Ctrl+↵. To insert a hard return [HRt], press Shift+↵. To insert a tab ([Left Tab]), press Ctrl+Tab.

To Control the ↵ Key

When creating or editing a style in the Contents box, you can control the behavior of the ↵ key as follows:

- To have ↵ insert a hard return without turning the style off, deselect (clear) Enter Key Will Chain To (for Character and Paragraph styles only).

- To have ↵ move the cursor past a style and turn the style on again, select Enter Key Will Chain To and choose <Same Style> from the drop-down list.

- To have ↵ move the cursor past the style, select Enter Key Will Chain To and choose <None> from the drop-down list.

- To have ↵ move the cursor past the style, then turn on another style, select Enter Key Will Chain To and choose the style you want to turn on next from the drop-down list.

OPTIONS   These style types are available:

Character (paired)   Like most paired codes, formats any number of characters between the [Char Style] codes. You can usually turn off a character style by pressing → .

Paragraph (paired)   Formats text from the cursor position to the first hard return that it finds. Usually, pressing ↵ turns a paragraph style off and back on again. To turn the style off, press Alt+F8 and apply the <None> style.

Document (open)   Useful for formats that affect an entire document. Once turned on, a document style stays on until some other style (or code) takes over.

These additional options are available in the Style List dialog box (Layout ➤ Styles):

QuickCreate   Copies basic formatting codes from the cursor position into a new style. After choosing this option, specify the style name, description, and type and choose OK.

Edit   Lets you edit the highlighted style. You can also edit a style by turning on Reveal Codes (Alt+F3) and double-clicking the appropriate style code in the Reveal Codes window.

Options   Leads to these options: Setup (lets you choose which styles appear in the Style List and where style changes are stored); Copy (lets you copy the highlighted style to the current document, current template, or supplemental template); Delete (deletes the highlighted style); Reset (resets the highlighted system style to its default codes); Retrieve (lets you retrieve system styles, user-defined styles, or both from a saved file or style library); Save As (lets you save system styles, user-defined styles, or both to a style library file).

NOTES   Styles can be saved to the current document (default), default template, or supplemental template.

Style lists in subdocuments are combined into the master document.

SEE ALSO   *Codes, Master Document, Outline, Preferences, Quick Format, Template*

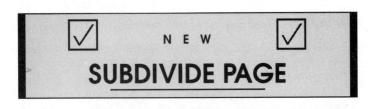

You can subdivide pages into columns and rows (rectangles). Each rectangle is treated as a separate page. For example, each sheet of 8 ½"× 11" paper that's divided into three columns and four rows will contain 12 rectangles, with each rectangle treated as a separate page.

Entering text on subdivided pages is similar to entering text on labels. You can see this effect in Page view and Two-Page view.

To Subdivide Pages

1. Choose Layout ➤ Page ➤ Subdivide Page.

2. Specify the Number Of Columns you want.

3. Specify the Number Of Rows you want.

4. Choose OK.

To Edit Text on a Subdivided Page

- Type and edit text normally. WordPerfect will start a new "page" automatically when the current page is filled.

- To force a new rectangle (page) to appear at the cursor position, press Ctrl+↵ (Page Break).

- To move the cursor from page to page, press Alt+PgUp and Alt+PgDn, or use any feature described in the Go To entry.

To Turn Off Subdivided Pages

- Move the cursor to where you want to disable the feature, then choose Layout ➤ Page ➤ Subdivide Page ➤ Off.

uppress   **203**

 NOTES   If you wish to reduce the margins on subdivided pages, choose Layout ➤ Margins.

To add borders or fill patterns to every square, choose Layout ➤ Page ➤ Border/Fill.

SEE ALSO   *Booklets and Pamphlets, Go To, Labels, Margins, Page Breaks, View*

SUPPRESS

You can turn off (suppress) automatic page numbering or repeating elements (headers, footers, or watermarks) to prevent them from appearing on the current page.

To Suppress Page Numbering or Repeating Elements

1. Position the cursor where you want to suppress the feature.

2. Choose Layout ➤ Page ➤ Suppress, or click the Suppress button in the Page button bar.

3. Select (check) whatever feature(s) you want to suppress, or choose All to suppress all features at once.

4. If you've turned on automatic page numbering and want to print a page number at the bottom center of the page, select Print Page Number At Bottom Center On Current Page.

5. Choose OK.

To Turn the Suppressed Features Back On

- Deselect the appropriate check boxes, or remove the appropriate [Suppress] code in Reveal Codes.

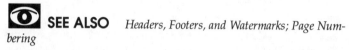 **SEE ALSO** *Headers, Footers, and Watermarks; Page Numbering*

TABLE OF AUTHORITIES

A Table of Authorities (ToA) is a list of citations in a legal document. The table is typically divided into sections according to the type of citation (Cases, Constitutional Provisions, Authorities, etc.). The document itself generally contains a *full form* citation (the first reference in the document) and a *short form* citation (an abbreviated way to show all subsequent references to the same authority).

To Display or Hide the ToA Feature Bar

Table of Authorities features are available when the Table of Authorities feature bar is visible.

- To display the feature bar, choose <u>T</u>ools ➤ Table of <u>A</u>uthorities.

- To hide the feature bar, click the <u>C</u>lose button in the feature bar.

To Set Up Citations

Repeat these steps for each authority that you cite:

1. Use the full form procedure to mark the full-form citation of the authority, edit the full-form text (if necessary), and assign a "nickname" (the short form) to that authority.

2. Use the short form procedure to mark all remaining references to the same authority.

After marking all the citations, define the appearance and location of each section of the table, then generate the table.

To Mark a Full Form Citation

1. Display the ToA feature bar.

2. Select the long form of the citation.

3. Click the Create Full Form button in the feature bar.

4. In the Section Name text box, type in a section name where the citation will appear or choose a section name from the drop-down list.

5. In the Short Form text box, type in or accept the suggested short form name (the short form name must be unique to this full form).

6. Choose OK.

7. Edit the full form text that appears in a new editing window. If necessary, you can use the Short Form and Section boxes in the feature bar to reassign the short form name or section. Choose Close when you're done editing the full form.

To change the full form citation later, click the Edit Full Form button in the ToA feature bar, highlight the short form name of the citation and choose OK (or double-click the name). Repeat step 7 above.

To Mark a Short Form Citation

1. Display the ToA feature bar.

2. Select the short form you want to mark from the Short Form drop-down list in the feature bar.

3. Position the cursor just after the short form text you want to mark. (You can choose Edit ➤ Find or press F2 to locate text quickly.)

4. Choose Mark from the feature bar.

5. Repeat steps 3 and 4 for the remaining short forms of this citation in the document.

To Define the ToA

1. Display the ToA feature bar.

2. Move the cursor to where you want the section to appear.

3. Optionally, press Ctrl+↵ to insert a page break.

4. Optionally, type a section heading and press ↵.

5. Click the Define button in the feature bar.

6. Optionally, do one of the following to create, edit, or delete ToA sections:

- To *change the definition* of a section, highlight the section name and choose Edit. You can change the name and any appearance options you want (see Options, below). Choose OK.

- To *create a new ToA definition*, choose Create. In the Name box, type a name for the section. Choose any appearance options you want. Choose OK.

- To *delete a section definition*, highlight the section and choose Delete.

- To *retrieve a list* of section definitions from another document, choose Retrieve, specify the document name, and choose OK. Select (check) the definitions to include and choose OK.

7. To insert the section definition into the document at the cursor location, highlight the section name and choose Insert.

8. Repeat steps 2–7 for each section in the ToA.

9. Optionally, use Page Numbering (Layout ➤ Page ➤ Numbering ➤ Value) to restart page numbering for pages that follow the ToA.

To Generate the ToA

1. Choose <u>T</u>ools ➤ Ge<u>n</u>erate from the menu bar, press
Ctrl+F9, or click <u>G</u>enerate in the Table of Authorities feature bar.

2. Choose OK.

OPTIONS You can choose any of the options below when creating or editing a ToA section definition:

Name The ToA Section name.

Position Lets you define where the page number appears
with respect to the text of the citation.

Page Numbering Lets you define the format of the page
number.

Underlining Allowed When selected (checked), any underlining in the text you marked will be included in the ToA. When
deselected, underlining is removed in the ToA.

Use Dash To Show Consecutive Pages When selected
(checked), a dash indicates consecutive page numbers. When
deselected, each page number in a range is listed separately.

Use As Default Uses the format of the current section as the
default for new sections.

Change Lets you change the style of the heading and subheading entries.

NOTES You can create a ToA for an individual document or a master document, but be sure to place the ToA definition in the master document, *not* in a subdocument.

To delete a citation entry, turn on Reveal Codes (Alt+F3) and delete
the appropriate [ToA] code. Then regenerate the ToA.

SEE ALSO *Find, Generate, Index, List, Master Document,
Page Numbering, Table of Contents*

TABLE OF CONTENTS

You can create a table of contents with up to five levels of indentation. This involves three basic steps. First, mark table of contents entries in your document. Second, define the table of contents location, number of levels, and appearance. Third, generate the table of contents.

To Display or Hide the ToC Feature Bar

Table of Contents features are available when the Table of Contents feature bar is visible.

- To display the feature bar, choose Tools ➤ Table of Contents.

- To hide the feature bar, choose the Close button in the feature bar.

To Mark ToC Entries

1. Display the Table of Contents feature bar.

2. Select the word or phrase you want to include in the ToC. (You can choose Edit ➤ Find or press F2 to locate words and phrases quickly.)

3. Click the Mark *n* button in the feature bar to assign the text to a table of contents level (*n* is a level number from 1 to 5).

Repeat steps 2 and 3 until you've marked all the entries you want.

To Define the ToC

1. Move the cursor to where you want the table of contents to appear (usually at the start of your document).

2. Optionally, type a title for the table of contents and press ↵.

3. Display the Table of Contents feature bar.

4. Click the Define button in the feature bar.

5. Choose formatting options from the Define Table Of Contents dialog box. You can define the number of levels and the appearance of each level in the ToC (see Options, below).

6. Choose OK to return to the document window.

7. Optionally, press Ctrl+↵ to insert a page break.

8. Optionally, use Page Numbering (Layout ➤ Page ➤ Numbering ➤ Value) to restart page numbering for pages that follow the ToC.

To Generate the ToC

1. Choose Tools ➤ Generate from the menu bar, press Ctrl+F9, or click Generate in the Table of Contents feature bar.

2. Choose OK.

OPTIONS   Choose any of these formatting options in the Define Table of Contents dialog box.

Number Of Levels (1–5)   Specifies the number of levels to include in the ToC.

Position   Lets you define where the page number appears with respect to the text of the table of contents entry.

Page Numbering   Lets you define the format of the page number.

Styles   Lets you change the style for each level of the ToC.

Display Last Level In Wrapped Format   Select (check) to wrap the lowest level of the ToC. Deselect to prevent wrapping.

NOTES   To delete a table of contents entry in the document, turn on Reveal Codes (Alt+F3) and delete the appropriate [Mrk Txt ToC] code. Then regenerate the ToC.

⊙ SEE ALSO   *Find, Generate, Index, Lists, Master Document, Page Numbering, Styles, Table of Authorities*

TABLES

The tables feature lets you organize text and pictures into neat rows and columns. You can also add shading and lines to emphasize parts of the table, and you can remove all or some of the lines, as in the examples presented below.

To Create a Table

- Choose Table ➤ Create or press F12, specify the number of Columns and Rows you want, and choose OK.

- Alternatively, you can move the mouse pointer to the Table Quick Create button in the power bar and then click and drag out a table with the number of columns and rows you want.

To Type in a Table

Move the cursor into the table and type normally. To move the cursor within the table, click any cell with your mouse pointer or use the Tab, Shift+Tab, Alt+←, Alt+ →, Alt+↑, Alt+↓, and arrow keys.

To Select Text within a Table

Drag the mouse pointer through the cells you want to select, or hold down the Shift key while using the cursor-positioning keys.

To Select Table Cells, Columns, or the Entire Table

1. Move the mouse pointer to any line within the table until the pointer becomes a vertical or horizontal arrow.

2. Do one of the following:

    *   To select the cell, click once.
    *   To select the row or column, click twice (double-click).
    *   To select the entire table, click three times (triple-click).

To Resize Columns

1. Move the mouse pointer to the vertical line that's just to the right of the column you want to resize. The mouse pointer will change to cross-hairs.

2. Drag the column line to the left (to narrow the column) or to the right (to widen the column). The Position indicator at the right side of the status bar will indicate the current position of the line as you drag.

3. When the column is the desired width, release the mouse button.

To size columns more precisely:

1. Move the cursor into the column you want to resize, or select the columns you want to resize.

2. Choose Table ➤ Format ➤ Column, or press Ctrl+F12 and choose Column.

3. Set the Width option to the width you want. If you do not want the column(s) to change size to accommodate changes to the width of other columns, select (check) Fixed Width. You can also increase or decrease the Left and Right margins within the column(s).

To Insert Rows and Columns

• To insert a row above the current row, press Alt+Ins.

• To insert a row below the current row, press Alt+Shift+Ins or move the cursor to the last cell in the table and press Tab.

• To insert several rows or columns, move the cursor to where you want to insert row(s) or column(s) and choose Table ➤ Insert (or right-click the table and choose Insert). Specify the number of Columns or Rows to insert and whether you want them placed Before or After the cursor position. Choose OK.

To Delete Rows and Columns

- To delete the row at the current cursor position, press Alt+Del.

- To delete several rows or columns, move the cursor to where you want to delete row(s) or columns(s) and choose Table ➤ Delete (or right-click the table and choose Delete). Specify the number of Columns or Rows to delete or whether to delete the Cell Contents of the current cell only. Choose OK.

If you make a mistake, use Edit ➤ Undo (or Ctrl+Z) to fix it.

To Format a Table

1. Position the cursor in the cell, column, row, or table you want to reformat, or select the cells, columns, or rows you want.

2. Choose Table ➤ Format, press Ctrl+F12, or right-click the table and choose Format from the QuickMenu.

3. Choose how much of the table you want to format: Cell (includes all selected cells), Column, Row, or Table.

4. Choose Alignment, Appearance, and other options as appropriate from the dialog box that appears.

5. Choose OK.

To Change Table Lines and Shading

1. Select whichever cells contain lines that you want to change.

2. Choose Table ➤ Lines/Fill, press Shift+F12, or right-click the table and choose Lines/Fill from the QuickMenu.

3. Choose Current Cell Or Selection to change lines in the selected cell(s) only, or choose Table to change the lines for the entire table.

4. Choose from among the various line styles, colors, and fill options to get the look you want.

5. Choose OK to return to the document.

To Delete a Table or Its Contents

Select the entire table (move the mouse pointer to a line in a table, and when it changes to a vertical or horizontal arrow, triple-click). Then press Delete (Del). Choose from among the following deletion options, then choose OK:

Entire Table Deletes the entire table, including its contents.

Table Contents Empties all the cells in the table, but leaves the table structure intact.

Table Structure (Leave Text) Deletes the lines and other table codes, but leaves the contents of the table intact. Rows will be separated by hard returns; columns will be separated by [Left Tab] codes.

Convert To Merge Data File Converts the entire table to merge data file records.

Convert To Merge Data File (First Row Becomes Field Names) Converts the second row and remaining rows of the table to merge data file records. The first row is converted to field names.

NOTES Because the Tab and Shift+Tab keys move the cursor from cell to cell, they don't play their normal roles when the cursor is in a table. To tab (indent) within a table cell, press Ctrl+Tab. To insert a back tab, press Ctrl+Shift+Tab.

There are several shortcut tools for creating and formatting a table. To get to a QuickMenu of table commands, right-click the table. To get to the Tables Button Bar, first activate the button bar if none is visible (choose View ➤ Button Bar), then right-click the current button bar and choose Tables from the QuickMenu that appears.

The order (or precedence) in table formatting is as follows:

Table Changes made at the Table level affect the entire table, but will be overridden by any other type of formatting.

Row/Column   Any formatting changes that you make at the Row or Column level will override formatting changes made at the Table level.

Cell   Any formatting changes you make at the Cell level override changes made at the Table, Column, and Row levels.

Other   Any changes you make within a table using the regular menus and shortcut keys (such as changing the font) override all of the above. That is, hidden codes within a table cell take precedence over any formatting changes made by going through the Table commands.

 SEE ALSO   *Columns, Table Math*

TABLE MATH

WordPerfect tables can be used as spreadsheets, to display numbers, and to perform calculations. If you're familiar with spreadsheet programs, you'll be able to learn the Table Math features quickly.

The Table Math features are easiest to use if you turn on the Table Formula feature bar.

To Display the Table Formula Feature Bar

Choose Table ➤ Formula Bar. When you're done using the feature bar, click its Close button.

To Put Numbers into a Table

Type the numbers into their cells in the document window.

To Put a Formula or Function into a Table Cell

1. Select (check) Table ➤ Cell Formula Entry. When Cell Formula Entry is selected, WordPerfect will try to calculate any numbers and formulas that you type into a cell.

2. Move the cursor into the cell where you want the formula, then type in the formula or function (using the correct format and rules for the function).

3. Move the cursor to another cell to see the calculation result.

To resume normal data entry (where numbers and formulas are treated as text and aren't calculated), deselect Table ➤ Cell Formula Entry.

To Enter a Formula or Function
Via the Table Formula Feature Bar

1. Turn on the Table Formula feature bar.

2. Move the cursor to the table cell where you want to enter the function or formula.

3. Do one of the following:

- Type the formula into the Edit Formula text box (using the correct format and rules for the formula or function).

- To select a function from a dialog box, click the Functions button. If you want to limit the list of functions, choose an option from the List Functions pop-up button (your choices are All, Arithmetic, Calendar, Financial, Logical, Miscellaneous, and Text). Highlight the function you want in the Functions list, choose Insert, then fill in any options required for the formula.

4. Click the Insert (✓) button in the feature bar.

To Point to a Cell or Range

1.   Turn on the Table Formula feature bar.

2.   In the Formula Entry text box, type all or part of the formula or function that will include the cell or range (if necessary).

3.   Position the cursor in the Edit Formula text box where you want the text to appear, or select the text you want to replace.

4.   In the document window, click on or select the table cell or range you want, or click on a floating cell in the document window.

5.   Finish typing the formula (as necessary), and click the Insert (✓) button in the feature bar.

To Sum a Row or Column

1.   Position the cursor at the bottom of the column or at the end of the row of numbers you want to sum. (To sum a row, the cell above the row must either be empty or must contain text.)

2.   Click the Sum button in the Table Formula feature bar, press Ctrl+=, or choose Table ➤ Sum.

To Copy a Table Formula

1.   Position the cursor in the cell that contains the formula you want to copy.

2.   Click the Copy Formula button in the Table Formula feature bar, or choose Table ➤ Copy Formula.

3.   Choose the Destination (To Cell, Down a specified number of times, or to the Right a specified number of times).

4.   Choose OK.

You can also use Data Fill (described next) to copy formulas.

To Fill Table Cells with a Formula or Pattern of Data

1. Establish the pattern you want, as follows:

   • *To establish an incrementing pattern* with Roman numerals, days of the week, months of the year, or quarters,
   type the starting value in the *first* cell of the range. *Examples:* **II** (Roman numeral 2), **Saturday** (day of the
   week), **February** (month of the year), **Qtr1 or Quarter1**
   (quarter of the year).

   • *To establish an incrementing pattern of numbers*, or a decre-
   menting pattern of numbers, Roman numerals, days of
   the week, months of the year, or quarters, type values into
   the *first two* cells of the range. *Examples:* To increment
   numbers by 20, starting at 100, type **100** in cell A1 and **120**
   in cell A2. To decrement the numbers by 20, starting at
   100, type **100 in cell A1 and 80** in cell A2.

   • *To repeat a single number, text value, or formula, t*ype the
   value into the *first* cell of the range. Formula cells will
   be adjusted automatically, unless you use absolute cell
   addresses (see Notes, below).

2. Select the cell(s) you entered in step 1, plus any cells that
   should continue the pattern.

3. Choose T<u>a</u>ble ➤ Data <u>F</u>ill from the menu bar, or press
   Ctrl+Shift+F12. You can also click the <u>D</u>ata Fill button in
   the Table Formula feature bar, or right-click the selected
   cells and choose D<u>a</u>ta Fill from the QuickMenu.

To Recalculate One or More Tables

Do any of the following:

• To calculate the current table or all tables in the document,
choose T<u>a</u>ble ➤ <u>C</u>alculate, then click <u>C</u>alc Table or C<u>a</u>lc
Document. Clicking the Calc<u>u</u>late button in the Table
Formula feature bar will also recalculate all tables in the
document.

- To turn automatic calculation on, choose T**a**ble ➤ C**a**lcu-
  late, choose either Calculate **T**able or Calculate **D**ocument,
  then choose OK.

- To turn automatic calculation off, choose T**a**ble ➤ C**a**lcu-
  late ➤ **O**ff and choose OK.

To Add a Floating Cell to Your Document

1. Turn on Cell Formula Entry, and display the Table
Formula feature bar if you wish.

2. Position the cursor where you want the floating cell to appear (the cursor must be outside of any table or floating cell).

3. Choose T**a**ble ➤ **C**reate ➤ **F**loating Cell, then choose OK.

4. Enter your formula, then move the cursor outside the
floating cell (for example, press →).

To edit the floating cell later, turn on Reveal Codes (Alt+F3), move
the cursor between the [Flt Cell] paired codes, and make your
changes.

NOTES The intersection of a column and row in a table
is called a *cell*. You use cell *addresses* to reference a specific cell in
formulas. In cell addresses, columns have letter names (A, B, C, D,
and so on), and rows are numbered (1, 2, 3, 4, and so on). For example, the address of the first cell in the table is A1. The address of the
cell in the third column and fourth row is C4.

A *range* is a rectangular group cells defined from an upper-left
cell to a lower-right cell. Use a colon or period to separate the
two cell addresses in a range. For example, B1:C8 or B1.C8 defines the range of cells from B1 (the upper-left cell) to C8 (the
lower-right cell).

You can also use *names* to name tables, floating cells, cells, ranges,
columns, and rows. Names can be used in formulas and functions,
as an alternative to addresses. To create named ranges, and perform other operations on named ranges, choose T**a**ble ➤ **N**ames or
click the **N**ames button in the Table Formula feature bar.

A *floating cell* is a formula or number, placed within the document text and enclosed in a pair of [Flt Cell] codes. Floating cells can contain any formulas, text, or numbers that table cells can, and they can reference table cells and other floating cells.

When you copy a formula, its cell addresses are usually adjusted to accommodate the formula's new position in the table. To prevent adjustment of a cell address when you copy formulas, enclose in square brackets the portion of the address that you don't want adjusted. *Examples:* [B]1 (keep the column number constant), B[1] (keep the row number constant), [B1] (keep the entire cell address constant). Cell addresses that can be adjusted during a copy are called *relative addresses*. Those that can't be adjusted are called *absolute addresses*.

When entering the text argument into the formula, enclose the text in double quotation marks. For example, **UPPER ("this is text".)**

 SEE ALSO   *Tables*

TABS

WordPerfect gives you two ways to set tabs: from the Tab Set dialog box or from the ruler bar. These tab types are available: Left, Center, Right, and Decimal (with or without dot leaders).

To Set Tab Stops with the Ruler Bar

1. Turn on the ruler bar (View ➤ Ruler Bar or Alt+Shift+F3).

2. Move the cursor to the start of the text where you want to change the tab settings, or select a block of text.

3. Use any method below to add, change, or delete tab settings.

- To *delete a tab stop*, drag the tab marker to below the ruler bar and release the mouse button.

- To *select several tab markers at once*, hold down the Shift key, move the mouse pointer to an empty spot just to the left of the first tab marker you want to select, then drag across the ruler to highlight the tab markers you want to select.

- To *delete several tab markers at once*, select the tab markers, drag the selected tab markers down below the ruler bar, then release the mouse button and the Shift key.

- To *move several tab markers at once*, select the tab markers drag the selected tab markers across the ruler bar to their new position, then release the mouse button and the Shift key.

- To *copy several tab markers to a new position on the ruler bar*, hold down Ctrl and Shift while selecting multiple tab markers. While still pressing Ctrl and Shift, drag the selected tab markers across the ruler bar to their new position, then release the mouse button and the Ctrl and Shift keys.

- To *delete all tab stops*, right-click the bottom of the ruler bar (where the tab markers are) and choose Clear All Tabs from the QuickMenu. Or, choose Clear All Tabs from the pull-down menu on the Tab Set button in the power bar.

- To *select a tab type* (alignment), right-click the bottom of the ruler bar and select a tab type from the QuickMenu. Or, select a tab type from the pull-down menu on the Tab Set button in the power bar.

- To *set a new tab stop*, select the tab type you want, then click on the ruler bar where you want the new tab to appear.

- To *change the type* of an existing tab stop, delete the tab stop, then set a new tab stop.

- To *move a tab stop*, drag it to a new position on the ruler bar. As you drag the tab marker, the right edge of the status bar will show the exact tab position. A *ruler guide* will also indicate where the tab marker is with respect to the text in your document.

- If, while dragging a tab marker, you want to return the marker to its *original position*, drag the marker above the ruler bar, then release the mouse button.

To Use the Set Tabs Dialog Box

1. Move the cursor to where you want to change the tab settings, or select a block of text.

2. Choose Layout ➤ Line ➤ Tab Set to open the Tab Set dialog box. (You can also right-click the ruler bar and choose Tab Set, double-click a tab marker in the ruler bar, double-click the Tab Set button in the power bar, double-click an existing [Tab Set] code, or click the Tab Set button in the Layout button bar.)

3. Use any method below to set a tab:

- To *choose how you want to position tabs*, choose either Left Margin (Relative) or Left Edge Of Paper (Absolute).

- To *delete all tab stops*, choose the Clear All button.

- To *delete one tab stop*, choose Position and type the position of the tab stop you want to delete. Then choose the Clear button.

- To *set default tab stops* (left tab stops every one-half inch), choose the Default button.

- To *select a tab type* (alignment), choose a tab type from the Type drop-down list button. Your choices are Left, Center, Right, Decimal, Dot Left, Dot Center, Dot Right, and Dot Decimal.

- To set *equally spaced tab stops*, select the tab type you want to repeat. Choose Position and type in the position for the first tab stop. Select (check) Repeat Every, press Tab, then type the distance you want between tabs. Choose the Set button.

- To *set one tab stop*, select the tab type you want. Choose Position and type in the position for the new tab stop. Make sure Repeat Every is deselected, then choose the Set button.

- To *change the type* of one or more tab stops, follow the procedure above for setting equally-spaced tab stops or one tab stop.

- To *move a tab stop*, delete the tab stop, then set a new tab stop at the spot you want.

4. Choose OK when you're done making changes.

NOTES Use tabs or indents, rather than spaces, to align vertical rows of text or to indent text by a precise amount of space. Tabs are initially set at every 0.5 inches.

Tabs indent to the next tab stop, with text wrapping back to the left margins. Indents temporarily change the left or left and right margins, with text wrapping to the tab stop (see the Indent entry).

Tabs move the cursor to the next cell in tables or to the next level in outlines.

SEE ALSO *Center, Decimal Alignment, Indent, Outline, Styles, Tables*

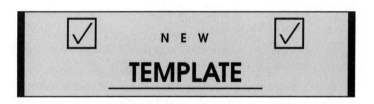

N E W

TEMPLATE

Every new document that you create is formatted according to an underlying template file. Templates establish the initial document text and available abbreviations, button bars, macros, menus, keyboards, preferences, and styles.

To Choose a Template
When You Create a File

1. Choose File ➤ Template (Ctrl+T).

2. Highlight the template you want.

3. Optionally, choose View to preview the template text.

4. Choose OK.

A new document window will open. All text and objects defined for the template will be available to you.

To Create a Template

1. Choose File ➤ Template (Ctrl+T).

2. Choose Options ➤ Create Template.

3. In the Name text box, type a name for the template.

4. In the Description text box, type a description.

5. To base the new template on an existing template, choose an existing template name from the Name drop-down list.

6. To preview the objects currently defined for the template, choose Objects.

7. Choose OK. A new window will open and the Template feature bar will appear.

8. Type the text, enter formatting codes, and choose feature bar buttons as needed. (See Options, below.)

9. To save the changes and return to the document window, choose Exit Template ➤ Yes.

To Edit or Delete a Template

1. Choose File ➤ Template (Ctrl+T), then highlight the template you want.

2.　Choose Options, then do one of the following:

- To delete the template, choose Delete Template ➤ Yes.
- To edit the template, choose Edit Template. Continue with step 8 of the procedure above for creating a template.

OPTIONS　These buttons are available on the Template feature bar:

Create Object　Lets you create a new template object (Style, Macro, Abbreviations, Button Bar, Keyboard, or Menu Bar).

Copy/Remove Object　Lets you copy objects from a specified template to the current template, or remove objects from the current template.

Associate　Lets you establish a connection between a template object and various WordPerfect modes or features. You can also run (trigger) a macro that's stored with the template when certain events occur. For example, a macro could display some instructions just after you create a new file based on the template.

Description　Lets you change the description for the current template.

Initial Style　Lets you define the initial style (InitialStyle) for documents created with this template.

Exit Template　Lets you save changes to the template and return to the document window.

NOTES　WordPerfect comes with several built-in templates. The *default template* (typically STANDARD.WPT) is used unless you choose a different template via File ➤ Template. The *supplemental template* is used as a source of additional styles.

To change the default or supplemental template location, choose File ➤ Preferences and double-click File. Choose Templates. Specify the default and supplemental directory and file names and the default template file extension (usually WPT), as needed. Choose OK, then choose Close.

SEE ALSO *Abbreviations, Button Bar, File Management, Initial Codes Style, Macros, Menus, Preferences, Styles*

TEXTART

Use WordPerfect's TextArt feature to add outlines and shadows to text, fill text with patterns and colors, pour text into any of 40 shapes, rotate text, and produce other special effects.

To Create a TextArt Graphic

1. Move the cursor to where you want to put the TextArt graphic.

2. Choose Graphics ➤ TextArt, or click the TextArt button in the WordPerfect button bar.

3. In the Enter Text text box, type the text that you want to stylize.

4. If necessary, choose Redraw to display your text.

5. Choose a font, style, justification, shape, color, outline, shadow, rotation, and any other options as desired.

6. Repeat steps 4 and 5 until you get exactly the look you want.

7. When you're happy with your creation, choose File ➤ Exit & Return To WordPerfect. When prompted, choose Yes if you want to save your changes.

To Edit a TextArt Graphic

1. Double-click the graphic you want to change, or right-click the graphic and choose Edit TextArt Object from the QuickMenu.

2. Repeat steps 3–7 of the procedure for creating a TextArt graphic (described just above) to change the image as needed.

OPTIONS The TextArt menu bar offers the options described below:

File Lets you create a new TextArt file, open a previously saved TextArt file, update the image in the WordPerfect document, save the image as a file on disk, print the image and set up the printer, and return to your WordPerfect document.

Edit Provides an Undo (Ctrl+Z) option for undoing changes made in TextArt, and a Copy (Ctrl+C) option for copying the image to the Clipboard.

ReDraw Lets you set redraw to Manual or Automatic (the default). With manual redraw, you must click the Redraw button to see the updated text. With automatic redraw (Auto), the text is updated whenever you make a change (this can be slow).

Help Provides detailed help with TextArt. You can also get help by pressing Shift+F1 and clicking on an area of the dialog box that you want to know more about.

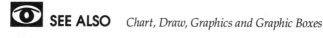 **NOTES** For a quick reminder about how to use a tool or text box in TextArt, move the mouse pointer to the area you're interested in. A description will appear at the bottom of the TextArt dialog box.

The embellished text is placed in a graphics box. You can size and position that box using all the standard techniques described in the Graphics and Graphic Boxes entry.

You can also use WP Draw to curve and embellish text. See the Draw entry.

SEE ALSO *Chart, Draw, Graphics and Graphic Boxes*

THESAURUS

Thesaurus lists and substitutes synonyms (words with the same or similar meaning) and antonyms (words with the opposite meaning) for words in your document.

To Look Up a Word

1. Position the cursor on a word you want to look up.

2. Choose Tools ➤ Thesaurus (Alt+F1), or click the Thesaurus button on the power bar. If the word you chose is in the Thesaurus, WordPerfect will list words with similar or opposite meanings.

3. To replace the word in your document with a word from the list, highlight the word in the list and choose Replace. To look up a new word, enter the new word in the Word text box, and choose Look Up. To return to your document without changing the original word, choose Close.

OPTIONS

<< and >> Use these buttons to scroll back and forth between lists of words.

Dictionary Lets you specify another Thesaurus dictionary file if you have purchased and installed one.

Edit Lets you cut, copy, and paste between the Word text box and the Clipboard, select all text in the Word text box, and undo your last action in Thesaurus.

History Displays a list of words you have looked up recently.

NOTES The Thesaurus screen displays *headwords*, *references*, and *subgroups*. A headword is a word you can look up. References are divided into nouns (n), verbs (v), adjectives (a), and antonyms (ant). References marked with a bullet (•) lead to additional headwords and references. References may be divided into subgroups, which are groups of words that share the same basic meaning.

To look up a reference word marked with a bullet, double-click that word, or highlight it and press ↵. Thesaurus will display the listing for that word in the next available column.

To activate a different column listing, click the mouse on the new column or press ← or →.

To scroll to references *within* a displayed column, use the mouse or the vertical cursor movement keys.

 SEE ALSO   *Speller*

TYPESETTING

WordPerfect's Typesetting options include many features used in desktop publishing and typesetting applications. Use them to get precise control over the text in your document.

To Adjust Typesetting Features

1. Move the cursor to where the typesetting options should take effect, or select a block of text (Word/Letterspacing only).

2. Choose Layout ➤ Typesetting.

3. Do one of the following:

    • To advance text up or down, choose Advance (see the Advance entry).

    • To create overstrike characters (characters printed one atop the other), choose Overstrike (see the Overstrike entry).

- To enter special commands for your printer, choose Printer Command and type the command or specify a file name that contains printer commands. If you want to insert a code that pauses printing temporarily, at the cursor position, select Pause Printer. Choose OK.

- To choose word spacing, letterspacing, justification limits, leading adjustments, automatic kerning, and baseline placement for typesetting, choose Word/Letterspacing. See Options, below.

- To kern two letters manually, choose Manual Kerning (see the Kerning entry).

4. Fill in any dialog boxes that appear, then choose OK.

OPTIONS The Word/Letterspacing options are described below:

Normal For word spacing and letterspacing respectively, spaces words or letters according to the specifications set by the font or printer manufacturer.

WordPerfect Optimal Spaces words and letters according to the specifications that WordPerfect considers best.

Percent Of Optimal Lets you specify the spacing width by entering a percentage of the Optimal setting. Percentages greater than 100 increase spacing between words or letters; percentages less than 100 decrease spacing. After selecting a Percent Of Optimal option, you can choose Set Pitch. The Set Pitch options let you specify the pitch in characters per inch (this is converted to a percentage of Optimal). Larger pitches decrease spacing between words or letters; smaller pitches increase it.

Compressed To Lets you adjust a percentage (0–100) for compressing the spacing between fully-justified words. By default, WordPerfect will compress spacing between fully-justified words to no less than 60 percent of normal.

Expanded To Lets you adjust a percentage (100–9999) for expanding the spacing between fully-justified words. By default, WordPerfect will expand the spacing between fully-justified words to no more than 400 percent of normal. (1000 or more allows unlimited expansion).

Adjust Leading   Select (check) this option, then specify the distance you want Between Lines separated by soft and hard returns.

Automatic Kerning   Select (check) this option to reduce excessive white space between certain letter pairs. The pairs of letters that WordPerfect can kern automatically are predefined for each font.

Baseline Placement For Typesetting   When deselected (the default), the *top* of the first line of text is aligned with the top margin. When selected (checked) the *bottom* of the first text line is aligned with the top margin. Selecting this option ensures that the bottom (baseline) of the first text line appears in the same place regardless of font or style.

NOTES   Once a word spacing limit is reached, spacing is adjusted between letters.

To restore settings to the defaults, turn on Reveal Codes (Alt+F3) and delete the appropriate code.

SEE ALSO   *Advance, Codes, Justification, Kerning, Line Height, Overstrike, Units of Measure*

UNDELETE

The Undelete command restores deleted text (including any codes within that text) at the current cursor position. You can use this feature to move text as well as to restore it to its previous position. WordPerfect remembers the last three deletions, and you can display or restore any one of them.

To Undelete Text

1. Position the cursor where you want to restore the deleted text or codes.

2. Choose Edit ➤ Undelete (Ctrl+Shift+Z).

3. The most recent deletion will appear in reverse video.

4. Do one of the following:

    - To restore the highlighted text, choose Restore.
    - To display the next oldest deletion, choose Previous.
    - To display a more recent deletion, choose Next.
    - To return to the document window without restoring, choose Cancel or press Esc.

 NOTES   While in the document window, you can undelete any of the last three deletions as long as WordPerfect isn't carrying out a command. Use Undelete if you accidentally deleted text or codes, or use it to quickly move or copy previously deleted text or codes.

A *deletion* is any group of characters and codes that you delete *before* moving the cursor to another place in your document.

You cannot undelete paired codes (e.g., [Bold]) deleted with the Delete or Backspace key. However, you can use Edit ➤ Undo or press Ctrl+Z to restore paired codes, if you do so immediately after deleting the codes.

SEE ALSO   *Cancel, Delete, Undo*

UNDO

The Undo command reverses the most recent change made to a document. This is a lifesaver!

To Undo an Operation

• Choose <u>E</u>dit ➤ <u>U</u>ndo or press Ctrl+Z.

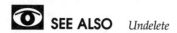 **SEE ALSO**   *Undelete*

UNITS OF MEASURE

WordPerfect uses measurements to position text and graphics on a page. The status bar displays the vertical and horizontal position of the cursor according to the current units of measure. The ruler divisions also reflect the current units of measure.

You can specify measurements in inches, centimeters, millimeters, points, or 1200ths of an inch.

To Change the Default Units of Measure

1. Choose <u>F</u>ile ➤ Pr<u>e</u>ferences and double-click <u>D</u>isplay.

2. Choose units of measure as follows:

• To set the units for the document window and dialog boxes, choose an option from the Units O<u>f</u> Measure pop-up list button.

• To set the units displayed on the status bar and ruler bar, choose an option from the Status Bar/Ruler Bar Displa<u>y</u> pop-up list button.

3. Choose OK and <u>C</u>lose.

 NOTES   Inches are the default unit of measure.

Whenever WordPerfect prompts for a measurement, you can enter
either fractions (3½) or decimal numbers (3.5).

WordPerfect uses the default units when you *omit* the units of measure. To temporarily override the default units of measure, *include* the
units of measure abbreviation (e.g., **12p** for 12 points). Abbreviations
are " or *i* (inches), *c* (centimeters), *m* (millimeters), *p* (points), and *1*
(1200ths of an inch). The entry will be converted to the default unit of
measure.

Although WordPerfect displays up to three numbers to the right of
the decimal point, it actually calculates up to six places.

SEE ALSO   *Document Window, Preferences, Ruler, Status Bar*

VIEW

You can view the pages of your document in three ways: Draft,
Page, or Two-Page view. You can also edit your document in any of
these views.

To Choose a View

1.   Choose <u>V</u>iew.

2.   Select one of these options:

• To view the document without page headers, footers,
watermarks, footnotes, endnotes, and other page
formatting features, choose <u>D</u>raft. (The shortcut key
for Draft view is Ctrl+F5.)

• To see a one-page view of the document with all page
formatting features, choose <u>P</u>age. (The shortcut key for
Page view is Alt+F5.)

- To see a two-page view of the document with all page formatting features, choose T̲wo-Page.

 NOTES There is no Print Preview in version 6 of WordPerfect.

The zoom, ruler, and Reveal Codes features aren't available in Two-Page view.

SEE ALSO *Document Window, Zoom*

WINDOWS

The W̲indow pull-down menu and various buttons and borders on windows let you open, close, size, position, and select windows. WordPerfect for Windows runs in its own *application window*. Each document you edit is in a *document window* (see the Document Window entry).

You can use standard Windows techniques and the W̲indow menu to size, position, and switch to various windows. See your Windows documentation for details.

NOTES The F̲ile ➤ O̲pen (Ctrl+O), F̲ile ➤ N̲ew (Ctrl+N), and F̲ile ➤ Template (Ctrl+T) commands open a new document window. F̲ile ➤ C̲lose (Ctrl+F4) closes an active window (see the Save/Save As entry).

You must activate (click on) a window before you can edit its contents. The title bar of the current (active) window is usually colored differently from the other (unselected) windows that are also open on the screen.

SEE ALSO *Combine Documents, Dialog Boxes, Document Window, Menus, Save/Save As*

ZOOM

Use Zoom to specify the magnification of on-screen text and graphics.

To Change the Zoom Magnification

Use either of the methods below:

- Choose View ➤ Zoom or double-click the Zoom button in the power bar to open the Zoom dialog box. Select a predefined size, or choose Other and enter a percentage magnification. Choose OK.

- Choose a magnification by dragging the highlight to the desired magnification on the Zoom button in the power bar.

To Change the Default Zoom Magnification

1. Choose File ➤ Preferences and double-click Display.

2. Choose View/Zoom.

3. Select a zoom percentage or enter one in the Other text box.

4. Choose OK, then choose Close.

 SEE ALSO   *Power Bar, Preferences, View*

INDEX

Note to the reader: Throughout this index, **boldfaced** page numbers indicate primary discussions of a topic. *Italicized* page numbers indicate illustrations.

SYMBOLS

& (AND) selection operator, 187
• (bullet), in Thesaurus screen, 228
✓ (check mark), in menus, 128
↵ (Enter) key, 91, 200
… (ellipsis), in menus, 128
➤ (triangle), xiii, 128
<> (not equal) selection operator, 187
< (less than) selection operator, 187
= (equal) selection operator, 187
> (greater than) selection operator, 187
? button, in feature bar, 56–57
\ (OR) selection operator, 187

A

abbreviations, xvii, **1–2**
absolute addresses, 220
active document window, 48
addresses, for table cells, 219
Adobe Type Manager, 63
Advance feature, **2–4**, 229
alignment character, changing, 39
Alt key, 127
anchor options, 73
AND (&) selection operator, 187
antonyms, 228
Append command, **4**
application window, 235
applications, starting automatically, 104
Arrange menu (WP Draw), 51
arrow (➤), xiii, 128
ascending sort order, 186
ASCII delimited text files, 134
  default settings for, 132
  importing, 195, 196
associate option, for template, 225
Attributes menu (WP Draw), 51
attributes of text, 62
automatic hyphenation, **85–86**
automatic kerning, 231
automatic links, 141
automatic numbering, *See* outline
automatic redraw, in TextArt, 227
automatic style, for outline, 147, 150
auto-replace, xxi

B

Back Tab, 123, 214
Backspace key, 41, 97
balanced newspaper columns, 23

Bar Codes, xx, **5**
baseline, distance between, 110–111
baseline placement for typesetting, 231
beep
  for hyphenation help, 89
  for misspelled words, 194
binding, **5–7**
binding offset, removing, 6
blank lines
  including in line numbering, 113
  inserting, 97–98
block protect, 23, 102, 103
block of text
  centering, 16
  converting to comment, 27
  deleting, 41
  dragging and dropping, 49
  keeping together, **102–103**
  replacing selected, 97, 183
body text, in outline, 149
booklets, xx, **7–9**, 166
Bookmarks, xvii, **9–11**
  cursor movement to, 10, 68
  hypertext jump to, 83
borders, xvii
  of graphics box, 71–72
  for pages, 8
  for paragraphs, 158
  for subdivided pages, 203
bullet (•), in Thesaurus screen, 228
bulleted indented lists, 90–91
bullets, inserting, 98
Bullets and Numbers feature, **11–13**
button bar, **13–14**
  for Chart, 20
  Chart button, 19
  displaying or hiding, 13
  Draw button, 50
  hiding, **82**
  for macros, 117, 121
  moving and sizing, 14
  outline, 146
  preference options, 164
buttons, determining function, 13

C

cancel, **15**
  menu choice, 127
Cancel button, 44
capitalization, Speller check for, 192, 194
captions, 72

238 Index

246 Index

U

Undelete command, 42, **231–232**
  to move codes, 178
UNDELETE command (DOS), 43
underlining, in table of authorities, 207
Undo command, **232–233**
units of measure, **233–234**
  preferences options, 163
unselecting, selected text, 184
updating
  chart, 20
  data links, 140, 196
uppercase characters, converting to, 29
user input, to merge, 132
user interface, xxi

V

version, of WordPerfect, 80
vertical lines, 75
  in headers and footers, 77
vertically centering text, 17
vertically moving text, 2–4
View button, 60
View menu, **234–235**
  ➤ Button Bar, 13, 117, 146
  ➤ Hidden Text, 81
  ➤ Hide Bars, 82
  ➤ Power Bar, 24, 161
  ➤ Reveal Codes, 22, 177
  ➤ Ruler Bar, 24, 180, 220
  ➤ Status Bar, 197
  ➤ Two Page, 7
  ➤ Zoom, 236
View menu (WP Draw), 51
view modes, xxi. *See also* screen display
  default setting, 163
Viewer window, 143
volume numbers, 154
  in headers and footers, 77

W

watermarks, xix, **76–78**
  suppressing, 203
.WCM file name extension, 121
white space. *See also* margins
  adjusting between letters, 103
  between paragraphs, 111, 157
Wide form paper option, 156
widow/orphan protection, 102
width of table columns, 212
wildcard patterns
  in search and replace, 176
  in Speller word, 195
Window menu, 235
  ➤ Cascade, 48

  ➤ Tile, 48
Window menu (WP Draw), 51
windows, **235**
  for documents, **48**
Windows (Microsoft)
  Common User Access (CUA)
      conventions, 126
  Control Panel, mouse customization,
      137
  Program Manager, File menu ➤ Run,
      99
  Sound Recorder, 190
  starting, xv
WordPerfect Optimal word/letterspac-
    ing, 230
WordPerfect for Windows
  closing, 55
  installing, xiv–xv, 98–100
  keyboards, xv
  new features, xvii–xxii
  save before exit, 181, 184
  starting, xv, 99
  system requirements, xiv
  version, 80
words
  adding to dictionary, 192
  cursor movement between, 35
  deleting, 41
  finding, 61
  hard or soft spaces between, 191
  search and replace for, 176
  selecting, 136
  spacing, 230
  Speller check for repeated, 192, 194
WP Chart 2.1 Object, ➤ Annotate, 21
WP.LRS language resource file, 110
.WPD file extension, 142
WPSPELUS.SUP dictionary, 193
WPUS.LEX dictionary, 193
WPWIN 6.0 keyboard, xv
WP{WP}.BK*n* file, 46
writing style, 68
writing tools
  disabling or enabling, 110, 195
  preference options, 164

Z

Zoom, xxi, 235, **236**
  default setting, 163

Common WordPerfect 6 for Windows Features

Feature	How to Get There	Feature	How to Get There
Line (graphic)	*See* Graphics Line	Open Document	Ctrl+O
Line Height	Alt+L LH	Outline	Alt+T O
Links (DDE & OLE)	Alt+E L	Page Numbering	Alt+L PN
Lists	Alt+T I	Page View	Alt+F5
Macro (edit)	Alt+T ME	Paper Size	Alt+L PS
Macro (play)	Alt+F10	Paragraph Formatting	Alt+L AF
Macro (record)	Ctrl+F10	Password Protect	F3 Alt+P
Mail	Alt+F M	Paste from Clipboard	Ctrl+V, Alt+E S, or Shift+Ins
Margins	Ctrl+F8	Path Name (insert in text)	Alt+I OP
Merge Documents	Shift+F9	Power bar (show/hide)	Alt+V O
New Document	Ctrl+N	Preferences (customize)	Alt+F E
Object (edit)*	Alt+E O or double-click object	Print/Fax Document	F5 or Ctrl+P
Object (insert embedded)	Alt+I J	QuickFinder (indexer)	Alt+F Q
Object Link (create)	Select previously saved object in server, copy to Clipboard, switch to WordPerfect, press Alt+E S, highlight linkable format, press Alt+L	QuickList (edit/display)	Ctrl+O Alt+L space
		QuickMark (set, find)	Ctrl+Shift+Q and Ctrl+Q, respectively
		QuickMenu	Right-click the mouse
		Repeat Next	Alt+E A